TRACKSIDE

East of the Hudson
1941 - 1953
with
William J. McChesney

by Jeremy F. Plant

with Brian D. Plant

Published by
Morning Sun Books, Inc.
9 Pheasant Lane
Scotch Plains, NJ 07076

Library of Congress
Catalog Card No. 97-075965

First Printing
ISBN 1-878887-89-0

Color separation and printing by
The Kutztown Publishing Co., Inc.
Kutztown, Pennsylvania

Acknowledgments

When Bob Yanosey first showed me a sample of Bill McChesney's photographic work, it was immediately apparent that Mr. McChesney's early color work would be a landmark contribution to the pictorial history of railroading in the Northeast. Not only was the time period of the photographs remarkably early for amateur color photography, but there was an unmistakeable style that unified the shots of different railroads and different settings. First off, Mr. McChesney was an action photographer: there are relatively few standing shots, and the action shots convey a feeling of movement and drama. Second, notice the compositions, especially in the steam shots where smoke plumes more often than not are an integral part of the scene. This isn't easy! Also of note is the way Mr. McChesney was able to include the train crew as part of the scene, humanizing the shot. When Bob Yanosey explained the forthcoming *Trackside* series of books featuring the work of the foremost color rail photographers in America, we agreed that Bill was a natural candidate for a book featuring his magnificent coverage of some of the great railroads of New York and New England in their finest years, between 1941 and the end of steam in the early 1950s.

Like many of the early slide photographers, Mr. McChesney did not include a great deal of information about each shot on the slide. His work was rarely if ever published. Fortunately, his son Peter was able to gather some information, but much detective work was necessary to pinpoint some of the locations and specific trains in the pictures that follow. Once again I am indebted to the libraries of the Pennsylvania State University, and the National Railway Historical Society for their assistance and collections. Mr. Donald S. Robinson provided valuable information on the Boston & Maine, and Mr. J. W. Swanberg on the New Haven. Elbert Simon provided useful information on the EAST WIND. Thanks also to my brother, Jeffrey G. Plant, for his general review of the photos, and of course to my partner on this project, my son Brian D. Plant, who fell in love with the material the moment he saw it and did much of the selection and arrangement of photographs, page layout, and some of the writing. Bob Yanosey was as always a source of encouragement and prudent advice–and someone who also recognized what a treasure trove the work of this pioneer slide photographer is.

Our greatest debt is to Peter McChesney, who appears in many of the photos as the little boy living out his dream of traveling around with his Dad, camping out near the tracks, riding the special trains, experiencing the thrill of participating in his father's passion. It's the same sort of experiences that Brian and I have had, and the chance to put together a book on another father-son team was a special privilege that will always have a great deal of meaning for us. Pete ensured that his father's collection would be considered in its entirety, and provided the information on the family history. He encouraged the project along in the most unselfish and helpful manner possible. The wish of both father and son was that others enjoy the pictures; and that, of course, is the whole purpose of a book like this.

JFP
Hershey, PA

TRACKSIDE *with* William J. McChesney

TABLE OF CONTENTS

TRACKSIDE

East of the Hudson 1941 - 1953
with
William J. McChesney

Bill McChesney holds a piece of rail acquired during one of his railroading excursions in the 1930s.

Bill McChesney was born in Summit, New Jersey on March 23, 1905. His father, William F. McChesney, worked in the gold and silver industry, rising to a senior executive position at the Gorham Company. To the best of the family's recollection, he had no special interest in railroads.

Bill grew up in Summit, an important suburban stop on the Lackawanna. He attended the Peddie School, graduating in 1923, and married Edith Smithers in his early 20s. Her father was a vice president of the Louisville & Nashville, and the opportunities presented by his position added to his growing interest in railroads.

While no one can pinpoint where, when and how his love affair with trains originates, it seems that Bill McChesney's active railfanning had three major sources: his childhood attraction to the Lackawanna trains passing through his hometown; his father-in-law's management position on a major railroad, the L&N; and his friendship with another Summit resident, John "Jack" Beach, who introduced him to photography.

Through his father-in-law, Bill was able to obtain passes to ride in the cabs of steamers on the Lackawanna, the Pennsylvania, and the New Haven. His son Peter relates one of his father's adventures. Bill rode a 1500 series Lackawanna 4-8-2 on the LACKAWANNA LIMITED from Hoboken to Scranton. Climbing down in a rather sooty condition from the cab of the steam engine, he was confronted by a member of the railroad police who accused him of being a stowaway on the flagship limited. He was greeted with much skepticism from the bull until he produced a pass signed by a Lackawanna VIP.

Friendship with Jack Beach enabled Bill to elevate his hobby from one of loving and riding trains to photograph-ing them. Jack Beach was a long-time friend who worked in the night photo lab of one of the New York City newspapers. An avid photographer, he got Bill interested in serious photography. Bill purchased a Leica in the 1920s, a time when 35 millimeter photography was much rarer than today. Not many particulars exist about this camera, which was sold a few years ago, but Bill's son remembers that he had an array of lenses and a separate light meter.

During the late 1920s and 1930s Bill lived in New Jersey, in Summit and Chatham, working in several jobs: for Gorham, in the banking industry before the Depression, and as one of the founders of the Hospital Service Plan of New Jersey, a precursor of Blue Cross and today's managed care.

Pete McChesney's interest in trains, like so many other children of his generation, was heightened by the thrill of a good old Lionel set running a loop around the living room rug. It's 1946 and Pete is four years old.

By 1951 steam was fast disappearing from Northeastern rails, and the McChesneys enjoyed the excursions that allowed the faithful to enjoy the last years of steam. Pete shows off his goggles for his photographer Dad that year.

After the outbreak of World War II, Jack Beach convinced his friend to help the war effort by becoming a safety engineer at the Aberdeen Proving Grounds in Maryland. Safety engineering was a relatively new profession, and it required Bill to take a six-month course at the Illinois Institute of Technology in Chicago before returning to Aberdeen.

In 1943, Bill moved his family to Connecticut and assumed a position as safety engineer with the Scovill Manufacturing Company in Waterbury. Waterbury in the war years was one of the most important manufacturing cities in the country, an essential part of the munitions industry centered in New England. Bill remained in Connecticut until retirement.

Upon retirement, Bill and his second wife, Jessie, moved to Martha's Vineyard where he was able to pursue a second hobby, carving and painting birds. He met one of the outstanding bird carvers, Wendell Gilley of Southwest Harbour, Maine, and emulated his work in fine-quality wood carvings for his own and others' enjoyment.

Bill's rail adventures in the postwar years were shared with his son, Pete, who appears in many of his rail pictures. The duo followed the trail of steam in its last glorious years in the East. Bill was also an avid model railroader, beginning with a large HO layout he shared with his brother-in-law, William Pott, in Summit in the 1930s. In Connecticut, he and Pete shared a large collection of Lionel equipment, returning to HO in the 1950s.

Some of these collections remain in the possession of the McChesney family to be enjoyed by future generations. Bill was also a talented artist, committing some of his rail images to pen and ink and charcoal drawings, as we see in this volume.

At the age of 92, Bill continues to live at Edgartown, MA with Jessie. He can be found touring Martha's Vineyard in an ancient red VW Rabbit and sharing his philosophy and experiences with a circle of friends and family.

Peter McChesney attended Northwestern University and moved to Ithaca, NY in 1964, where he directs a company that provides alumni relations and development services to colleges and universities in the Northeast. He has raised a family of six children, who, in his words, "...in this era of flight, were never fortunate enough to hear the wail of a steam whistle or to enjoy the luxury of a trip in a Pullman bedroom or to watch the snow swirl away behind the windows of an observation car."

Before beginning our photographic review of Bill McChesney's work, let's briefly review the rail scene in New York and New England in the decade between 1941 and 1951, when most of the shots in this book were taken.

No longer chasing steam together, Bill and Pete still find time for frequent reunions at Bill's home on Martha's Vineyard. It seems only yesterday that they were riding behind steam on the Rutland, camping out in the Hudson Highlands, and looking down at the New York Central as they slowly passed over the New Haven bridge at Poughkeepsie. Such wonderful memories!

Northeastern Railroads 1941-1953

Bill McChesney's color coverage of Eastern railroading began in the troubled years immediately before American involvement in World War II. For American railroads, it was a time of change, as the worst years of the Great Depression were put in the past, and the first diesels appeared, presaging a major change in motive power in the upcoming decade. In the East, the passage of the Transportation Act of 1940 put to rest finally the notion that the government, through the Interstate Commerce Commission, would create through forced merger four or five major Eastern systems built around the Pennsylvania, New York Central, Baltimore & Ohio, and various combinations of lesser roads. The new approach would stress a new type of partnership between the rail industry and the federal government, in which the railroads would continue to be regulated but would be free to pursue mergers of their own volition.

The low return on capital typical of the overbuilt and mature rail industry had led to a decline of interest in railroads on Wall Street. At the turn of the century, J. P. Morgan and his colleagues in the financial community had helped bring an end to what to them was ruinous competition in the rail industry, allowing railroad managers to concentrate on operations and technological innovation. Prevented from price competition by government regulations, unable to pursue mergers due to the ICC's desire to plan a national map for the industry, vulnerable to economic cycles and rising fixed costs, especially of labor, the rail industry no longer was the darling of Wall Street it had been a half-century before.

In the East, the big question was what would transpire in the way of consolidation once the industry was free to reorganize without a government plan to guide it. Clearly the region was overbuilt, and smaller trunk lines like the Erie and the Nickel Plate were outgunned by the giants, Pennsylvania and New York Central. In New England, the reliance of the New Haven on passenger revenues – around 45% in most years, the highest of any major road – and the continued question of whether and how the Pennsylvania would use its massive resources to influence the future of railroading in the region, given its historic interest in the New Haven, raised questions about the ability of the region's major roads to combine into a single trunk line. The Boston & Albany provided New York Central a major presence in the region not shared with any of the other non-New England Class Ones. The B&M had acquired control of the Maine Central in the 1930s, but had stopped short of total merger. The B&M remained dependent upon connections with other roads, and had a large system with relatively short hauls, causing some to label it a terminal railroad.

World War II gave the nation's railroads a tremendous boost. Both traffic levels and profits grew to record levels, often never to be repeated even in the boom years of the postwar economy. The war was very different from World War I, a European War that had put a strain on the Eastern roads where most of the troop and supply embarkations were centered. The effective use of submarines by the Germans menaced coastal traffic, putting commodities such as petroleum and bituminous coal that had moved by ship onto Eastern rails in record amounts. Revenues rose higher than profits, indicating that fixed costs, too, continued to rise, a menacing fact of life for an industry where the slightest economic downturn led to disaster.

Railroad management after the war was aggressive in two areas: using profits to retire as much fixed debt as they could, much of it left over from the bad years of the Depression; and modernization, primarily by converting to diesel power and by upgrading signalling and yard facilities. It was an exciting few years, with change the order of the day.

For the casual observer, the years between 1946 and 1953 gave little indication of the problems that dogged the industry. Most companies found the capital to improve their equipment and rolling stock; passenger travel held strong until the auto industry was able to satisfy the longing of the American public for new cars; even weak roads such as New Haven and Rutland had years of profits and optimistic hopes for the future. The years of Bill McChesney's greatest photographic activities, 1949-1951, were the peak years of investment in new equipment. Steam was being phased out in massive purchases of diesels, CTC and other signalling was replacing the old-time station operator, and the emphasis was on speedy time freights, fewer terminal delays, and longer runs.

For a steam lover like Bill, the region's rapid embrace of dieselization allowed no delays in seeking out the remaining steam operations. One by one, the New England and New York roads dieselized. By 1951, steam was on its way out on the New Haven, Rutland, D&H, and B&M. The B&M would keep its Moguls and Pacifics on branch line and commuter operations for a few years, but steam operations on mainline freights was almost over by the end of 1951. On the New York Central, the mountainous Boston & Albany was one of the first parts of the system to be dieselized. Only the sheer size of the job of dieselizing the nation's second railroad kept steam at work for a few more years in the early 1950s. The Korean War, the last twentieth century war in which the railroad system was expected to play the major role in transporting men and material, kept things going strong for another three years. But 1954 was a bad year, 1957 even worse for Eastern roads. Dieselization was complete, and it was time to turn to mergers before the ink turned red again.

It is fitting that Bill McChesney's rail photography, most of it unpublished, be the subject of one of the first in the *Trackside* series. Bill was an aficionado of the moving train, especially the steam powered train, out on the line, with smoke billowing and a river valley or coastline to set the mood and create a background. Although he shot extensively across North America, it is his work on the close-by lines of eastern New York and New England that form the core of his work. Bill also had the sense to get out and shoot before the railroad scene he had known was gone in the great changes sweeping across the railroad scene in the postwar years. All rail photographers sense instinctively that change is the only constant, that you have to get out and record the action before it's gone. Thankfully, Bill McChesney had the foresight to understand how fragile the rail scene of New York and New England was in the years just before and just after World War II. He had a Leica and color film when color photography was still rare and difficult. He had a son to travel with and share unforgettable scenes of Eastern railroading in its finest hour. Let's take a trip back to those exciting years, when America still relied on the railroad.

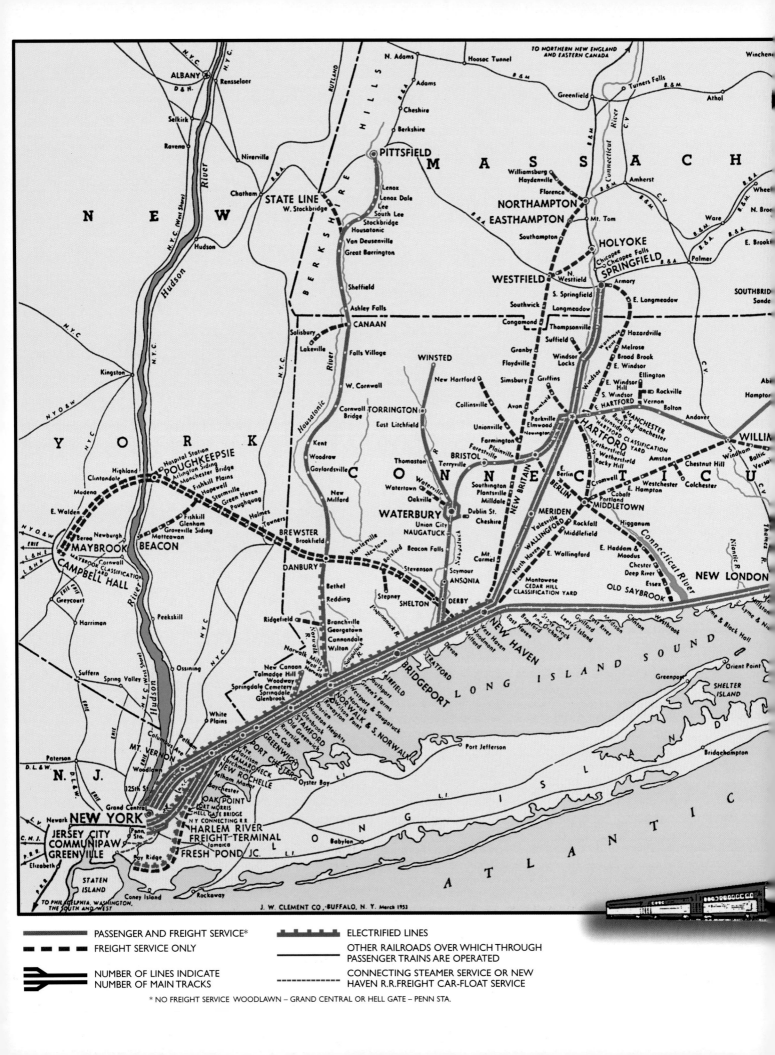

PASSENGER AND FREIGHT SERVICE*

FREIGHT SERVICE ONLY

NUMBER OF LINES INDICATE
NUMBER OF MAIN TRACKS

ELECTRIFIED LINES

OTHER RAILROADS OVER WHICH THROUGH
PASSENGER TRAINS ARE OPERATED

CONNECTING STEAMER SERVICE OR NEW
HAVEN R.R. FREIGHT CAR-FLOAT SERVICE

* NO FREIGHT SERVICE WOODLAWN – GRAND CENTRAL OR HELL GATE – PENN STA.

J. W. CLEMENT CO., BUFFALO, N. Y. March 1953

The New York New Haven and Hartford RAILROAD

Long Island

When Bill McChesney visited the Long Island Railroad in 1941, the 339 mile road was firmly under the control of the Pennsylvania Railroad. In 1928 the Pennsy had assumed operational control of the LIRR, its subsidiary and partner in the Penn Station project in Manhattan, having bought a controlling interest in the road in 1900. For such a large railroad, the Long Island was unique even in the Northeast in its reliance upon passenger service–it usually ranked first among major railroads in the percentage of revenues from passenger operations. It also operated wholly within New York State, connecting New York City with the small towns and farmland of Nassau and Suffolk counties in the days before the Island was transformed into a bedroom of New York. Connecting with its parent road at its western end, the Long Island's freight service was a long terminal operation, since it had the eastern counties of Long Island all to itself. The Long Island of 1941 was about to be sorely tested by the demands of war, as it had been during World War I, since Long Island had a large weapons industry and a number of military bases requiring special service; in addition, of course, the restrictions on driving will put virtually all commuters on the rails for the duration of the conflict.

(Above) The PRR years on the Long Island saw the senior road assigning a number of its steam engines to service on the Long Island, notably 4-4-2s and 4-6-2s made surplus by the electrification projects of the 1930s. On the last day of May, 1941, the most famous of the PRR steam types, a K-4s Pacific, has a morning westbound in tow at Canoe Place, NY, on the run from Montauk to New York. It is one of 425 members of Pennsy's most famous class of steam locomotives; around 70 saw service on the Long Island.

(Right) Bill's skill as an artist is evident in this masterful charcoal drawing of one of the Pennsylvania Railroad's big E-6s 4-4-2s, #68.

(Right) Overshadowed by their more famous K-4 successors, Pennsy's K-2 Pacifics never received much attention. But the K-2s were handsome pre-World War I era passenger engines, as shown by the 732 at an eastern Long Island location. Around nine of these early 4-6-2s saw service on the Long Island; the 732 was the lowest numbered of the group assigned to the Long Island.

(Below) The eastern end of Long Island before World War II was a coastal land of scrubby pines, potato fields, and small towns still far removed from the hustle and bustle of New York City. The winds of war are blowing toward American involvement in the global conflict as another K-4 slams by the semaphores at Hampton Bays near the eastern end of Long Island's southern shore. The date is October 25, 1941.

(*Right*) The E-6s Atlantics were by anyone's account one of the finest and most successful of their type anywhere. During the Pennsy years on the Long Island, they shared duties with the G class 4-6-0s and various classes of 4-6-2s on the numerous passenger runs of the island carrier. In October of 1941, one of their number shows off its chunky lines in this striking sidelit view at Canoe Place.

Built in 1914, when most other roads were switching away from the Atlantic to the 4-6-2 Pacific, the E-6s, over 80 of which were built, gave good service to owner Pennsy and leasor Long Island, 28 of which served at one time or another on the Long Island.

Hell Gate Bridge connecting the boroughs of Queens and the Bronx in New York City is the only rail link between Long Island and New England. Its opening in 1917 provided the first direct connection at Manhattan for passenger service between New England, New York, and points to the south and west on the Pennsylvania Railroad via Penn Station in Manhattan. We'll use Hell Gate as the symbol of our move eastward to New England. We begin by looking at the New Haven, the road synonymous with rail transportation in southern New England and one of Bill McChesney's favorite lines.

New Haven

WATERFORD TOWER

(Above) Bill often visited Waterford Tower, just west of New London, helping the towerman throw the switches and plan train movements over the busy Shore Line. His charcoal drawing illustrates the Armstrong switch throws and the view from the tower window. The area just to the west of the tower, between Niantic and Waterford, was Bill's favorite locale for shooting trains on the Shore Line.

The linchpin of transportation in southern New England until its absorption into Penn Central in 1968 was the New York, New Haven, & Hartford Railroad – the New Haven. Few railroads have had as colorful a history as this Yankee carrier. The New Haven was frequently a pawn in the often sordid, always cynical, occasionally hilarious, and ultimately depressing tale of greed and amorality played out by J. P. Morgan and his minions in the first years of the century. The New Haven was a great cash cow holding a virtual monopoly in the rich and developed territory it controlled, and the Morgan interests used it for every sort of shenanigan on the margins of legality they could think of. After the public and the government demanded change, around World War I, the Pennsylvania saw the New Haven as part of a scheme to penetrate east of New York City and ensure the movement of freight from their lines to New England by way of water transport from one side of New York harbor to the other. In bankruptcy during the Depression, the New Haven entered a period of receivership between 1935 and 1947 which in many ways was its golden era. Freed from the ravenous capitalists for a brief spell, the sober management under the receivers invested in the property, improved service, and benefitted from the enormous growth in traffic experienced during the war: freight service doubled and passenger service almost tripled, allowing the New Haven to salt away more than enough earnings to pay off its debt and re-emerge as a solvent rail corporation on September 18, 1947.

William McChesney moved his family to Connecticut in the mid-1940s, and saw the New Haven at its best, before another round of rapacious capitalists – the Dumaines, Patrick McGinnis, and George

Alpert – drove the road into another, and in this case terminal, bankruptcy. The New Haven we see in these following shots was still the Grand Dame of New England railroading, with a tradition of elegant passenger service between Boston, New York, and other New England cities; an innovative road with some of the first road freight diesels, piggyback freight service, and long distance electrification.

The area of the New Haven that most intrigued Bill was the Shore Line, the 156.8 mile stretch of mainline between New Haven and Boston. The portion of the Shore Line he found most alluring was the stretch between Madison and New London, where the tracks hugged the shoreline of Long Island Sound, especially the area between Old Saybrook and New London. The McChesneys owned a cottage in the area, and the New Haven was one of the roads that honored the Bill's pass, allowing him to visit the Shore Line in the exciting years between 1941 and the end of steam a decade later.

(Above) American Locomotive Company had traditionally been the builder of the New Haven's steam power, but Baldwin underbid the Schenectady company for the order of 10 streamlined 4-6-4s delivered in the first half of 1937. The I-5s were gorgeous and powerful, looking unlike anyone else's modern passenger power with their glossy black-and-silver paint, as shown here near Niantic with a westbound passenger train. It's August 1941 and the four-year-old I-5s are the rulers of the Boston-New Haven run, unthreatened as yet by the Alco DL-109s that will come on board in December of that year.

(Above) In a perfect combination of steam engine and smoke plume I-5 1403 heads the YANKEE CLIPPER westbound west of New London in August 1941. The tender shows off the silver New Haven script emblem that replaced the spelled-out road name that the I-5s wore upon delivery from Baldwin. The 1403 is in her home territory; the New Haven rarely used the 4-6-4s anywhere but the Boston-New Haven Shore Line. The CLIPPER was a New England institution, leaving the Hub City promptly at noon each day, passing New London a little after 2 PM, and into Grand Central at 4:30 PM, in time for dinner and theatre in New York.

(Left) In a location near Niantic that captures well the coastal feel of the Shore Line, one of its namesake 4-6-4s blasts by with a westbound express. In those days, South Station in Boston saw the hourly departure of one of New Haven's Shore Line expresses, from the 7 AM departure of the MURRAY HILL to the 6 PM start of the PERSHING SQUARE. The big 4-6-4s were powerful, smooth-riding, and highly dependable. Their streamlining was among the best ever applied to a modern steam engine, and since they were designed to be shrouded, the streamlining was done in such a way that it did not get in the way of normal maintenance. The I-5s were never de-streamlined, not even during the war years, a testament to the good design of the people at Baldwin.

(Above) Near the same location in Waterford double-headed I-4s charge west led by the 1354. This is the expensive practice that the New Haven largely eliminated with the more powerful I-5s, which were able to handle the long Shore Line expresses solo. Passenger service was a big business on the pre-war New Haven; every day saw 182 passenger trains operated, along with 220 freights; the daily count of passenger miles was four million.

(Below) Skirting the shore of Long Island Sound at Waterford, the 1375 heads east with the ISLANDER, headed from New York to Woods Hole, MA and the connection for the ferry to Nantucket. The train left New York at 2:45, passed New Haven at 4:18 and is due to the make the steamer connection at 8:30. This was also a seasonal train, running eastbound on Fridays between June 27 and August 29 and westbound on Sundays between June 29 and August 24, with the final New York-bound run on Monday, September 1. Since the train operated down the Old Colony to the Cape, it did not rate an I-5. In the years before the war the New England coast was one of the favored vacation destinations in the East, and the New Haven provided the best means to reach Maine, Cape Cod, the offshore islands, and the Connecticut shoreline. The green-over-red signal heralds the approach of a westbound on this busy line, perhaps the westbound PILGRIM due through here a little after 5 PM.

One of the most colorful trains ever to operate in New England was the EAST WIND between New York and the Maine coast. This unique yellow-and-silver train was a joint venture of the New Haven, Boston & Maine, Maine Central and Pennsylvania, the last road providing through service south of New York. The train operated via Worcester and the B&M's line from Worcester to Lowell Junction and up the Western Route to Portland. The idea was a speedy, daylight, all-coach train from Washington and New York to the Pine Tree State. Unlike the overnight BAR HARBOR EXPRESS, the EAST WIND allowed travelers to disembark at any of six Maine locations, with connections on the B&M for New Hampshire's White Mountains. The Pennsy contributed equipment painted canary yellow with silver striping and a broad silver window band; other equipment came from the New Haven and Atlantic Coast Line. The New Haven magazine **Along the Line** characterized it this way: "Strikingly decorated to provide a gay vacation atmosphere, the new train's silver and canary exterior will harmonize with bright interiors." The EAST WIND was strictly a seasonal train, running late June to September; its first run was June 21, 1940. Curiously, the Pennsy repainted the cars into standard PRR tuscan red for regular service each fall and back into the canary and silver each June. In the summer of 1941, when Bill took the following shots of the train, two lounge cars had joined the baggage cars and coaches on the train. All the equipment carried the train name on the side of the car. The "yellow train" lasted only from 1940 to 1942, so Bill's shots that glorious summer of 1941 around Waterford and Niantic are to be treasured.

(Above) I-4 1351 heads the matched consist westbound in August 1941. Trains like the EAST WIND heading directly to and from Maine used the Shore Line between New Haven and New London and the Norwich & Worcester Line between New London and Worcester. The nifty little train was due out of Bangor at 6:40 AM, into Worcester at 1:45 PM, and is due into New Haven at 4:41 PM, meaning it's around 4 PM as it heads along the shore near Niantic. New Haven, where the electric power took over for the run to New York, was the only scheduled stop on the New Haven's share of the run.

(Below) At one of Bill's favorite locations along Jordan Cove of Long Island Sound the EAST WIND heading to Maine meets the westbound SENATOR slamming by with an I-5 on the lead. Service to Maine via Worcester saved miles and time compared to a routing through Boston, and of course, saved the problem of transferring from South Station to North Station in Boston. All that's needed is a matching observation car! The train ran through from Washington via Penn Station, New York City, and the Hell Gate Bridge. All seats were reserved, and a reasonable special service charge of 80 cents was charged. That summer of 1941 the train ran from June 21 to September 27, the second year of its three year run with the canary yellow equipment.

(Below) Bill's fascination with the New Haven's classic I-4 Pacifics included artwork as well as photographs. I-4 1390 is portrayed catching the last instant of sunlight on its smokebox before it plunges into a tunnel with a consist of dark green heavyweight cars. This was the Shore Line in all its glory in the years before World War II.

(Right) The 4-6-2 Pacific type was the classic American passenger engine of the prewar era. At its best the Pacific combined grace, elegance and power. Nowhere was this more evident than on the New Haven, where the I-4 class was the culmination of the development of the 4-6-2 arrangement on a road that lived and died with its passenger service. The I-4 possessed a noble front-end design, as shown by the 1391 blasting westbound on the Shore Line with the westbound PURITAN near Niantic in August of 1941.

(Above) Although the Shore Line was Bill's favorite place to shoot the New Haven in 1941, he ventured over to the Maybrook Line on May 5 of that year to shoot lumbering Santa Fe type 3236 at Clintondale, NY. The 50 L-1 2-10-2s were the drag freight champions of the New Haven, especially suited to the heavy grades and tonnage of the line to Maybrook, NY. Built by Alco in 1918, this and its fellow 2-10-2s will shortly be put to the test as the war taxes the ability of the New Haven to keep moving over this vital route.

(Below) Another elderly freight hauler was Mikado 3013, seen at Norwood, MA. One of 25 J-1 2-8-2s built by Alco in 1916, by the 1940s the J-1s had been relegated to secondary freight service and other odd jobs around the New Haven.

(Above) Another old engine still active in the summer of 1941 was 2-6-0 270, seen at one of Bill's favorite locations near Waterford with the westbound local freight. She was one of 240 K-1 Moguls built between 1900 and 1907; less than 70 were still active when this shot was taken of the elderly Alco.

(Below) Switchers sometimes are neglected by photographers in search of the more glamorous road engines in action out on the line. The 0-8-0 type was favored by the New Haven along with most major roads for heavy switching duties. The workhorses of the system were the Y-3 class 0-8-0s delivered to the road in 1920 by Alco and built to USRA design. The 3406 sunning itself at Southampton Street in Boston was one of 35 Y-3s on the road. Like all USRA 0-8-0s she was built for power, not speed, with tiny 51" drivers. Good engines, the Y-3s lasted right up to the end of steam in the early 1950s.

New Haven entrusted most of its freights on the Shore Line to engines of the 4-8-2 wheel arrangement. Thank the government for introducing the type to the New Haven, in the form of the first ten of the United States Railway Administration's Light Mountains, built by Alco/Richmond in 1919 and given road class R-1 by the recipient road. The new engines were what the New Haven badly needed: modern fast freight power that could speed the tonnage over the Shore Line and other major arteries of the New Haven system. Pleased with the USRA machines, the New Haven ordered 30 near-duplicates in 1920; nine more arrived in 1924 for a total of 49. One of the 1920 machines, the 3314, is bearing down on us with a westbound Shore Line freight, its handsome front end highlighted by the slung Elesco feedwater heater, the pilot mounted air pumps, and passenger-style pilot. It's August 1941, and the R-1s are getting middle-aged and a bit weary.

(Above) In a beautifully composed scene an R-1 is heading east near Niantic. The goldenrods and golden grass in the meadow tell us that summer is nearing an end. The broadside angle of the 4-8-2 shows how modest the proportions of the USRA Mountains were, especially when equipped with the smaller tender this engine trails. These engines produced 53,900 pounds of tractive effort, enough to move freights on the moderately graded Shore Line, but insufficient for the grades of the Maybrook Line.

(Below) Backlit against the morning sky at 6:45 AM, an R-1 heads west with another Shore Line freight along the Connecticut coastline. Bill invested a good deal of time that August recording in color the last months of busy peacetime rail traffic on the New Haven, the end of steam's monopoly on the road. War and the DL-109s arrived almost simultaneously at year's end, beginning the swift downward slide for steam in southern New England.

(Above) A typical Shore Line freight of 1941 behind an R-1 is eastbound a few miles east of Niantic. The USRA 4-8-2 is laying down a nice black smoke plume this late summer day.

(Left) A different view is provided of the 3317 heading east along the Connecticut coastline with a late afternoon eastbound freight, another of the series of fine shots Bill McChesney produced in the late summer of 1941. Bill was 36 years of age then and a master of the new art of color slide photography.

(Above) Leaning into the curve with another Shore Line freight is one of the road's penultimate Mountains, R-3 3552, an Alco product of August 1926, showing off the look of the New Haven's modern 4-8-2s. In the 1920s Alco was trying to carve out a niche for itself with fast, powerful three cylinder freight engines, and the New Haven bit at the bait, ordering three R-3s in 1926 and 10 almost identical R-3-as two years later. As was the case with other roads, the third cylinder added greatly to maintenance problems, and the New Haven lacked the funds during the tough years of the 1930s to modify their balky 3500s. They hung on along with the other classes of New Haven steam until the big purchases of Alco cab units and road switchers made them expendable, in 1949-51. The 3552 shows off the distinctive sheet-metal air pump shield on its pilot that the R-3s wore for a number of years. The big compounds were rated for 5,500 tons on the New Haven-Boston run, around a 125 car train in those days.

(Above) Near Niantic an R-3 heads east in August 1941. This could be Cedar Hill to Worcester freight N-W2, due through Niantic around 4 PM bound for a 9 PM arrival at Worcester, or Greenville-Boston freight F-G-B2, through at roughly the same time. Maybrook-Boston trains O-B2 and O-B4 were also regular assignments for the three-cylinder 4-8-2s, but passed through this section of the Shore Line after dark.

(Right) In an unforgettable scene of steam railroading on the Shore Line, an R-3 speeds along the blue waters of the Sound, a perfect smoke plume accenting the speed of its passage, in August of 1941. The train is Massachusetts-bound in the morning of what promises to be a beautiful late summer day in New England, when the air first starts to hint of the coming of autumn. In these last days of the last summer before the war, who can guess the changes about to engulf the New Haven and all American railroading, or the enormous conflagration about to engulf Bill McChesney's generation?

(*Left*) Sparkling I-5 1401 passes light through returning to Boston from Cedar Hill after outshopping following a collision between it and a freight in 1947. One of the most beautiful and elegant steam engines ever built, it doesn't need a train or any props to dazzle the bystander.

(*Below*) The I-5s had a short period of dominance on the Shore Line. Alco passenger units, DL-109s and, after 1948, PA-1s bumped the I-5s by 1950. In the last years of operation the big Hudsons were more likely to be found on secondary assignments than top runs, such as the Boston-Providence local passing through Sharon Heights, MA in 1947 behind the 1405. The 44 miles between the capitals of Massachusetts and Rhode Island were the last to see the passage of the big 4-6-4s.

(Above) Another, considerably dirtier I-5 heads a longer consist under the semaphores at Sharon Heights. The small numberboards and inconspicuous numbers make identification of the I-5s in action shots difficult if not impossible.

(Below) Heading down to the races, an I-5 slams over the Neponset River bridge with a Narragansett Park extra, only a wisp of black smoke trailing over the train. The picture is undated but probably very close to the end of I-5 operations in 1950. The aluminum paint on the drivers, so much an identifying mark of the 4-6-4s, is barely discernible through the grime. The I-5s were the only really modern steam engines on the New Haven, and lasted less than 15 years, much less than that in the top-of-the-line passenger service they were designed to do.

(Above) In a location made famous by Kent Cochrane's marvelous shots of L-1 2-10-2s, Alco cab units in a perfect A-B-A configuration round the curve near Beacon Falls on the Naugatuck Line, headed for Waterbury in May 1949. Alco built 30 FA-1s, 15 FB-1s, and 5 FB-2s for the New Haven, forming the backbone of the road's road freight fleet until their gradual supercession by road switchers. Few color schemes were as breathtaking as the New Haven's orange.

(Left) In April 1949, orange FA 0403 leads a westbound freight around the blue waters of Niantic Bay. Niantic is derived from an Indian word meaning "point of land." Located in the town of East Lyme, Niantic was for centuries a center of shell-fishing, with an active scallop and clam fishing industry along the numerous inlets and salt flats of the Sound.

(Above) On September 10, 1950 a trio of almost-new RS-3s heads a Framingham extra at Walpole, MA The train has come down from Boston on the Old Colony and will head north on the Lowell line to Framingham. The New Haven rostered 45 RS-3s, bought between 1950 and 1952, and used them on about every type of assignment on the road, from passenger service to local freights to mainline assignments. It's rare to see NH RS-3s this clean: even the radiators are immaculate.

(Below) The 12 RS-1s delivered to the New Haven in 1948 were local freight engines primarily used on assignments like this westbound Shore Line local that Bill found at Madison, CT in August 1952.

(*Above*) New London's waterside station at the base of State Street provided the setting for a remarkable look at the Shore Line in the days of domination by Alco A-1-A cab units. Looking east, a two unit set of DL-109s led by the 0735 heads west with a freight. The units show the two color schemes applied to these vintage units, the lead unit wearing the Pullman green and yellow, the second the short-lived warm orange with silver pinstripes. Although the war is almost four years in the past, this scene reminds one when the 60 0700s provided much of the muscle needed by the New Haven to move the record amounts of freight compiled in those wartime years. The New Haven was by far the biggest purchaser of this Alco model, and with it pioneered the concept of diesel dual service locomotion.

(*Above*) Moving his Leica to the west, Bill found a set of newcomers. Two PA-1s led by the 0778 head an eastbound express into the station. The 0778 is part of a 17-unit order delivered earlier in 1949 to supplement 10 others bought in 1948 and delivered in the orange pinstriped scheme. One can almost smell the salt air blowing from the Sound at this, Connecticut's most maritime city, location of the Coast Guard Academy and the big submarine works on the Thames River. Careful study of this picture reveals the presence of the New Haven this day, with R-1b 4-8-2 3339 simmering at the waterside engine terminal, along with a set of DL-109s and an Alco switcher. In the distance, to the right of the ship's funnel, is visible the green and gold of another set of Alco cab units. New London's harbor, one of the finest in the East, stretches for three miles along the estuary of the Thames. The sunken river produced a harbor of great depth, enabling large vessels to enter safely. Settled in 1646, incorporated as a city in 1784, New London was once one of the largest whaling ports in the world, rivalling Massachusetts' New Bedford. By the 1940s the maritime business had been replaced by education, tourism, and submarine manufacturing as the economic bases of the attractive city.

(Above) Waiting for a local freight assignment, the 3339 shows off her USRA design by the blue water of the Thames. The 3339 was the last of 30 Mountains built by Alco in 1920 to USRA specifications, reflecting the success of the government agency's light mountain design on the Shore Line in the busy days just after World War I. These were the first fast, modern steam freight power on the New Haven. The Thames was originally called the Monhegin, in honor of the local Indian tribe that lived in the area, but was renamed at the time the name New London was chosen for what its backers hoped would become the greatest port of the New World.

(Above) Considering how rare the 2-8-2 wheel arrangement was on the New Haven, it's a testament to the usefulness of the J-1s that they lasted so long on the road. All 25 of the class were still around after the war had ended, making them candidates for last-run assignments like the 3013 all dolled up for the farewell to steam on the New Haven-Northampton Canal Line. Flying white extra flags and snazzy with silver cylinder heads and trim, the 1916 Alco is at Cheshire, CT in May 1949.

(Left) The New Haven's own PA-1s were not the only passenger engines from Alco to roam New Haven rails in the late 1940s. The AMERICAN FREEDOM TRAIN paid a visit to the New Haven as part of its nationwide tour in 1947-48, which began at Philadelphia on September 17, 1947. The train is seen at Waterbury station the first week of October in 1947. The scheduled stops for the train on the New Haven were at Bridgeport, Waterbury, Hartford, New Haven, and New London. By the end of its coast-to-coast voyage the train would log over 37,000 miles, bringing to the American public in their home towns the original Declaration of Independence, an early copy of the Constitution, and the Bill of Rights, among other historical artifacts. The train included cars equipped to display the documents, provided by the Pennsylvania Railroad and the Santa Fe, and domicile cars from Pullman to house the crews and the 24 Marine guards in full dress uniform who guarded the invaluable national treasures. The train was a testament to the safety and accessibility that the nation's rails provided for such a venture, co-sponsored by the Department of Justice and the American Heritage Foundation. At the end of the sojourn the locomotive was purchased by the Gulf, Mobile and Ohio Railroad.

(Left) Rocky Neck State Park on Long Island Sound is still months away from the busy summertime crowds of bathers and sunworshippers as a westbound express behind two PA-1s curves around the shore line on April 1, 1950. The 0770 was the first of the 17 of the 1949 order of PA-1s delivered in green and gold; the first ten, delivered in warm orange, regrettably were repainted into the green shortly thereafter.

(Above) Looking west, the 15 car train snakes around the gentle S curve at Rocky Neck and heads toward New Haven and New York. Long Island Sound is a long arm of the Atlantic, extending 90 miles from Throgs Neck at the entrance to New York's East River to the open ocean near the Rhode Island/Connecticut line.

(Above) Class I-2 Pacific 1312 is at Norwood Central, MA in 1952 with an Old Colony passenger run. The 50 I-2s were delivered to the New Haven in 1913 as top-of-line road passenger power, but were quickly displaced by the I-4s on the top runs, leaving them to work secondary and commuter runs for most of their long careers, especially on the Old Colony lines south of Boston. The longest careers belonged to 1312 and 1318, which lasted into 1952 as two of the last four active steam engines on the system.

(Below) One of the last assignments for the remaining New Haven steam engines in the late 1940s and into the 1950s was extras bound from Boston to Narragansett Park raceway in Rhode Island. I-4 1380 heads a holiday extra down to the races on July 4, 1951, a very late for New Haven steam, at Sharon Heights.

(Above) Southampton Street engine terminal in Boston is the setting for these broadside portraits of two other classes of New Haven 4-6-2s taken on July 7, 1951. The 1388 is one of 50 I-4 Pacifics the New Haven received from Alco in 1916. She will write the final chapter for New Haven steam in less than a year from the time of this photo, handling the last regularly scheduled train on March 11, 1952 and a final steam special on April 27 of that year. Look carefully and you will see that the 1388 has a center Boxpok driver and a large tender with six-wheel tender trucks.

(Below) Also at Southampton Street that summer day was I-1 1004, one of the last three of her type still extant at this late date for New Haven steam. She will not last out 1951, being retired in the fall of that year.

On April 29, 1951 Bill and Pete rode a special on the Old Colony lines of the New Haven. Leaving Boston's South Station at 9:15 AM, the train followed the main to Canton Junction, headed to Fall River and Newport, thence to Lowell via Mansfield and Framingham, returning via Walpole and Norwood for a scheduled 7:15 arrival back in Beantown. The cost was $3.60 for adults, a more-than-reasonable tariff for a full day's review of some of eastern New England's most interesting lines.

(Above) At Newport, RI I-1 Pacific 1004 poses for the photographers as their fellows search out every available source of elevation to record the event. The graceful machine was one of the first order of 4-6-2s placed by the road in 1907. Called "Grasshoppers" by the New Haven personnel in recognition of their outside Walschaerts valve gear, they were, as New Haven historian J. W. Swanberg notes, the steam engine that introduced the New Haven to modern motive power. Handsome and durable, the 73" drivered machines lasted on secondary passenger assignments (and even an occasional freight) until all were retired by the end of 1951. The 1004 was one of the last three to see service, but gave up the ghost in November 1951.

(Above) Riding the turntable at Newport, the I-1 shows off her unmistakeable New Haven lines, accented by the typical NH arched cab window. The sprightly Pacifics were one of the finest legacies of the Morgan-Mellen years of the New Haven.

(Below) In a scene not to be repeated for very long on the New Haven, the 1004 is watered under the supervision of a crew member whose service to the road is probably in the same range as the 44 year old Pacific.

(Above) At Framingham, the special pauses to allow the riders to view big I-4 4-6-2 1357 on the head of the Lowell-bound train. Framingham was the spot at which the NH's line to Lowell passed the Boston & Albany mainline between its two namesake cities. The NH line allowed the southern New England carrier to penetrate the industrial Merrimack River Valley, otherwise the exclusive territory of the Boston & Maine.

(Right) The stop at Framingham provided an opportunity for Pete McChesney to pose on the New Haven's H16-44 road switcher 561, built by Fairbanks-Morse in 1950 in the older style designed by Raymond Loewy.

(Above) Another interesting New Haven operation out of South Station, Boston, was the CRANBERRY to Cape Cod. DL-109 0722 was painted cranberry red and white, given a special nose emblem, and placed in service on the train to Hyannis in 1949. She kept the garb for four years, seen here on June 10, 1951 with an unmatching fellow DL-109.

(Above) Not too many railroads can say they had a train designed by a dirigible manufacturer – in fact, none can but the New Haven, which put its little one-of-a-kind three-car COMET in service between Boston and Providence in 1935. The blue and silver train was built by Goodyear Zeppelin in Akron, OH and powered by a 400 horsepower Westinghouse diesel engine in each of the two power cars. Its three cars seated 160 passengers. Placed in local service in the 1940s, it is back on its original run in this early 1950s shot leaving South Station. Given its experimental nature, the little COMET was more successful than many lightweights of the 1930s, and lasted a respectable 16 years in service before retirement in 1951 and subsequent scrapping.

(Below) A cutaway view of the little streamliner illustrates how well its designers integrated the two power cars with the passenger compartments. The art-deco era loved interiors of soft earth colors like the two-tone tan colors chosen to complement the blue and silver exterior. The COMET's two 400 horsepower diesels gave the train a healthy power-to-weight ratio and excellent performance. The artwork even highlights one of the more unusual features of the train, the "vertical pencil beam" light above the power car to warn motorists at grade crossings.

SPEED *and* SAFETY

Designed for speed—and rapid acceleration—The Comet was planned to be one of the *safest* trains in existence. Constructed of Duralumin, one of the strongest and lightest of metals, with the center of gravity nearly 25 inches lower than ordinary trains, it *hugs the rails*, develops little sway and makes curves imperceptible . . . yet it weighs less than half of a conventional type train with equal seating capacity.

Powerful headlights flood the tracks and a vertical pencil beam on the roof points skyward, warning motorists long before the long range sirens can be heard.

The latest type brakes, doors with folding steps in the center of the car, which must be closed before the train can move, combine with many innovations to give The New Haven the finest and the safest streamlined train the world has seen.

Introducing "THE COM

ULTRA-MODERN   AIR-CONDITIONED STREAMLINED TRAIN .. THE NEW HAVEN'S "COMET"

(Above) Advertising was growing in sophistication in the prewar years, and the brochure prepared to tout the new COMET was in keeping with the times. "Ultramodern" -- "the last word in luxury rail travel" -- "the world's finest streamlined train." As impressive as the little streamliner was, it never captured the New England imagination the way the streamliners did in the West, the ZEPHYRS of the Burlington and the CITY trains of the Union Pacific. Nor did it spawn a developing stable of streamliners to supplant the traditional steam-driven heavyweight trains on the Shore Line. It was an orphan by the war years, the precursor to the vain efforts of the New Haven in the McGinnis era to redress the decline of passenger service by lightweight gimmickry.

BEAUTY and COMFORT

Outside, the entire train is finished in two broad bands of blue, a lighter blue running along the window zone, and a darker blue along the "skirt". Between and above these color-bands, the entire length of the train is finished in a fascinating natural aluminum with a glistening whorled surface.

Inside are deep seats of extra width, low, without the need for footrests . . .

indirect lighting . . . air-conditioning, thermostatically controlled, with the warmed or cooled fresh air entering the car through slots near the ceiling . . . rubber inserts and insulation to obviate noise and vibration, specially designed shock absorbers . . . in fact, every device of modern engineering has been employed to make The Comet a thing of grace and beauty . . . a luxuriously comfortable new-type train.

ET" . . . last word in luxury rail travel —

New England railfans had it good in 1951, as a number of special trips afforded day trippers a chance to view the railroad operations in New England and nearby New York State. Bill was on board for the May 20, 1951 trip sponsored by the Connecticut Valley Chapter of the NRHS. Leaving New Haven in the morning, it traversed the Maybrook Line to that important New Haven yard in Orange County, NY, picking up additional passengers in Danbury along the way. For a fare of $4.75 from New Haven or $3.75 from Danbury, the throng got 270 rare and impressive miles, including a sidetrip from Maybrook to Middletown, NY over the New York, Ontario & Western.

(Left) The highlight of the trip was of course the Hudson River Bridge at Poughkeepsie. Looking south as the train obeyed the 12 miles per hour speed limit Bill captured this view of the hilly river city. Of interest are the New York Central's Hudson Division mainline, its passenger station and trainshed, and the nearby engine terminal with a number of the Central's 4-6-2s awaiting a call to return to Harmon with the frequent locals connecting the Hudson Valley communities with New York City.

(Below) A few months later, on September 30, 1951, Bill returned to Poughkeepsie to capture this classic shot of an A-B-A set of Alco-GE cab units crossing the big bridge with a westbound freight for Maybrook. By this time, the lumbering 2-10-2s that had once ruled this mountainous New Haven line were gone, and the covered wagons from Schenectady were in charge of freights on this most important bridge route to the west.

(Above) Returning to the May trip, it's a milky-cloudy day at Maybrook, as often seems to be the case with fantrips. Nonetheless, the giant interchange yard is a veritable cornucopia of rail wonders. First off, the engine terminal is full of Schenectady's best. Three unit sets of FA/FB Alcos in various combinations of Warm Orange and Hunter Green dominate the engine terminal, while little Lehigh & Hudson River offers a set of RS3s to complete the all-Alco scene.

(Right) Moving over to the hump on the east side of the yard, we see the engine terminal from another perspective. The special train's two Alco road switchers get some attention beside a Lima switcher, one of 10 of the 1200 horsepower units purchased from the Ohio builder in 1950 and commonly found at Maybrook. Check out those vintage reefers in the foreground.

(Right) Judging from the scanty attire of the brakeman riding the Pennsy X-29 boxcar down the incline, May 20 was a warm day. Maybrook was the New Haven's major connection with the Erie, the New York, Ontario & Western, the Lehigh & Hudson River, and Lehigh & New England, and the easiest way for freight moving to New England to bypass the congestion of New York City.

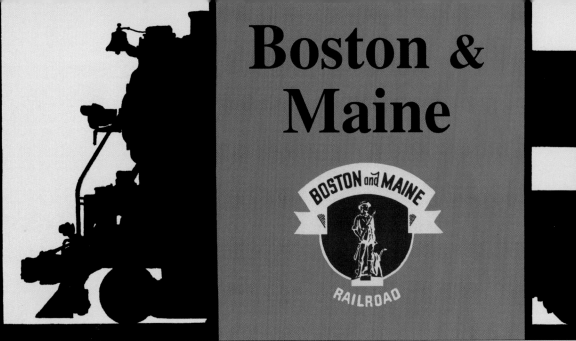

Boston & Maine

While the New Haven ruled supreme in the south of New England, the Boston & Maine dominated the northern tier of the region, with lines radiating north and west out of Boston to Portland, ME; Troy, NY; Bellows Falls and White River Junction, VT; and connections to Canada via the Canadian Pacific, Central Vermont, and Rutland. Described by New Englanders as a road from "somewhere to nowhere," the B&M didn't have the density of passenger service enjoyed by the New Haven in its populous New York/Boston corridor. What the B&M had was charm, class, and a distinctiveness far beyond its middling size among American railroads. Its major routes provided the major rail connection between Maine and the rest of the country, and a superior east-west bridge route by way of the great Hoosac Tunnel for traffic moving into and out from eastern New England. This great New England carrier is portrayed comprehensively in **Boston and Maine in Color** *by this same author published by Morning Sun. What we see in the next several pages is the B&M in transition in the postwar years, with colorful early diesels in the Minute Man scheme sharing its tracks with ancient 2-6-0s and a variety of 4-6-2s as the* Route of the Minute Man *forges ahead with a dieselization program that began before the war and wasn't completed until the summer of 1956.*

(Above) North Station in Boston was the hub of B&M passenger operations, where both commuters and intercity travelers accessed the New England metropolis. North Station was located near the Charles River on, fittingly, the north side of Boston. It featured four lift bridges over the Charles providing entry to 23 stub end tracks. In this panoramic view we are looking north over the Charles to the engine terminal and freight yard on the north side of the river. On the right an inbound commuter train is passing Tower A and crossing the river into the station behind one of the road's P-2 Pacifics. An E-7 waits in the terminal with an outbound intercity run. Note the large coaling tower across the river in the Boston engine terminal. This shot was taken from the high rise Hotel Manger adjacent to the station.

(Above) An unusual visitor to North Station in 1947 was EMD's TRAIN OF TOMORROW. The E-7-led streamliner toured the nation touting the postwar advances in rail passenger equipment. She is seen here parked on the west side of the station, with a DeSoto club coupe on Nashua Street comparing her 1940s lines with those of the blue and silver domeliner. The four-car train was the brainchild of EMD, who conceived of it as a traveling advertisement for postwar passenger diesel power and streamlined, vista-dome cars. The E-7 pulled four cars, each of a different type, illustrating the latest in car design. The *Star Dust* was a chair car, the *Sky View* a double-decked dining car, the *Dream Cloud* a luxurious sleeping car, and the *Moon Glow* an observation car; each had what GM called "Astradomes" atop them, identical 30' air-conditioned domes. Alas, New England would prove to be resistant to the sales pitch, and never saw regular domeliner service (with the exception of the CP's line across northern Maine).

(Below) A broadside shot of the 3235 shows its compact lines. The B&M purchased a great many engines in the period between the turn of the century and 1920, as it expanded its trackage through acquisition of smaller railroads and shared in the general increase of railroad traffic in these decades. The Atlantics were not more common on the B&M largely because the more favored Pacific type appeared only a few years later, and proved to be a great success. The 4-4-2s were the first engines on the B&M with trailing trucks, and were called "Trailers" by B&M men.

(Above) North Station was the scene of numerous railfan trips sponsored by the New England Rail Enthusiasts. On June 10, 1951, the rare duo of Mogul 1415 and Atlantic 3235 is putting out a nice display of steam in the cool morning air, waiting to take out a fantrip sponsored by the New England Railroad Enthusiast. The 1415 is one of the B&M's famous B-15 2-6-0s which provided a half-century of service to the road in branch line and commuter service. The 3235 is even rarer. One of 25 J-1b 4-4-2s built at Manchester in 1908-09, she is the last of her type in service on the B&M. This is one of the all-day jaunts favored by the Railroad Enthusiasts, a 260 mile circuit over a number of B&M lines. The trip headed west on the Fitchburg Division to South Ashburnham, MA, up the Cheshire Branch to Keene, NH, down the Ashuelot Branch to Dole Junction, down the Connecticut River Line to Greenfield, back over the Fitchburg to Gardner, down to Worcester and Clinton, and then back to Boston over the Central Massachusetts. The cost: $4.25 for adults.

(Above) Inbound morning commuter trains could be shot nicely from the east side of the tracks as they crossed by Tower A and the Charles River bridges. Engine 3638, a P-2-a 4-6-2 built by Alco in 1911, heads a typical commuter run of three wooden cars into Boston in August, 1952. This scene would be repeated many times daily until the end of steam in the summer of 1956.

(Below) At one time, North Station was a fairly major site for long-distance passenger runs. Passengers could depart for St. John, New Brunswick via the Maine Central and CP; for Troy, NY over the home road and on to points west on the New York Central; and for Montreal by three routes: the Rutland via Bellows Falls, the Central Vermont via White River Junction; and the CP via the connection at Wells River, VT. Two E units, B&M E-7 3817 and CP E-8 1800, wait to take a northbound to Montreal over the B&M/CP routing, up the New Hampshire Mainline to Concord, thence over the White Mountains Line to Woodsville, Wells River, Newport, and Montreal.

(Above) One of the 10 P-3-a Pacifics built for the B&M by Alco in 1923 shows off its red striping and shaded lettering at the Boston engine terminal. The P-3-a's were more common on intercity passenger runs than in commuter service, often found on the Connecticut River Line or on the lines radiating northwest from Boston to New Hampshire and Vermont. Note that this engine has been modernized with the addition of center Boxpok drivers.

(Below) Besides the usual plethora of P-2 Pacifics and 2-6-0s North Station also saw some unusual locomotives on a regular basis. Pacific 3699 waiting to head out of the station with a northbound run is one of four Class P-5-a 4-6-2s built by Brooks in 1924 for the Delaware, Lackawanna & Western for service on its secondary mainlines in New York State. Bought by the B&M during World War II, to help the road deal with the increase of passenger traffic occasioned by the conflict, they were well-liked by the road and lasted until 1952. Like the P-3-a's, they were more common on intercity runs than commuter service.

(Above) Another fantrip is about to depart from North Station behind steam power. B-15a Mogul 1488 is at the head of an excursion to New Hampshire on August 16, 1952. Again sponsored by the New England Division of the Railroad Enthusiasts, the special left Boston at 9 AM, traveled up the Eastern Route to Swampscott, then to Marblehead, Salem, Danvers, Wakefield Junction, Lawrence, Manchester, Portsmouth, Rockingham, and back to Boston on the Western Route. All in all, over 250 miles under steam, quite a bargain for $4.25.

(Left and opposite page) The 1488 is at the Manchester station with the special prior to heading out to Portsmouth. The old Mogul is no stranger to the pioneer industrial city along the Merrimack, having been constructed in the Manchester Works of Alco.

(Above) The B&M was a pioneer in dieselizing its mainline operations, beginning with the purchase of 24 A-B sets of FTs during World War II and continuing with the addition of 21 E-7s and an equal number of F-2s just after the conclusion of the conflict. The B&M embraced the road switcher idea early also, purchasing 10 RS-2s from Alco in 1948. The versatile RS-2s were the first of a large fleet of Alco road switch-ers put into service by B&M. Here the 1534 in the first road switcher scheme, with Minute Man emblem on the long hood nose and no black paint above the top separation stripe, heads a Connecticut River Line local near Northampton, MA on October 1, 1949. This promises to be one of those railfanning days that we dream of, with perfect cloudless weather and plenty of interesting trains.

(Left) Like many another railroad in the early 1950s, the B&M found the EMD GP-7 to be the finest of the early road switchers. Following on the heels of the spectacularly unsuccessful BL-2, which the B&M sampled with an order of four units in 1948, the GP-7 was much improved in appearance and versatility. The B&M purchased 23 between 1950 and 1953, assigning them at first to Boston area commuter service and other passenger assignments. In August 1952, Bill found the 1563 on the point of a local from Concord passing the Granite Street crossing in Manchester, NH. In the background can be seen the fine brick buildings formerly operated by the Manchester Locomotive Works of Alco, the birthplace of the B-15 Moguls and many other B&M steam locomotives. The manual crossing and shanty, as usual, are a gathering point for people to watch the trains pass.

(Above) More commonly assigned to the Conn River trains were the B&M's 21 F-2s. The B&M liked their FTs and moved after World War II to expand their fleet of EMD cab units by purchasing the 1350 horsepower F-2s in 1946. The 4224 set was a regular on the Conn River, seen here with the southbound train 74 at Charlestown, NH on October 1, 1949. The station continues to identify the stop as Charlestown, NH/Springfield, VT, but the electric trains of the Springfield Terminal now bring only freight to the interchange with the B&M; passenger service ended in 1947.

Bellows Falls, VT was an important junction for freight and passenger traffic in Northern New England in the postwar years. Situated at a spectacular point on the Connecticut River, Bellows Falls was the point at which the north-south Connecticut River Line, shared by the Central Vermont and B&M, met the Rutland's line from its namesake city and the B&M's Cheshire Branch from South Ashburnham on the road's Fitchburg mainline; together, the two lines formed an east-west routing for freight and passenger traffic between New England and points west. Cramped into a small space between the river and hills on both sides, the Bellows Falls area (including adjacent North Walpole, NH) featured trains from all three roads, a set of four diamonds, a ball signal to guard the crossing, and a handsome stone arch bridge over the Connecticut. Come visit Bellows Falls on October 1, 1949 courtesy of Bill McChesney.

(Above) The Boston section of the GREEN MOUNTAIN FLYER, train 3303, arrives at the Bellows Falls station behind P-4d Pacific 3716, *Roger's Ranger.* Like all the modern P-4s, the 3716 was built by Lima and named by New England schoolchildren with names out of the history of the region. The 3716 was named by Jean P. Beard of Hillsboro High in Hillsboro, NH. Readers of Kenneth Roberts's classic *Northwest Passage* will recognize the appropriateness of 3716's name to the upper reaches of the Connecticut River, the setting for the heroic exploits of Colonel Robert Rogers and his intrepid Rangers in the years of the French and Indian Wars.

(*Above*) Dropping its train off at the station for a waiting Rutland Ten Wheeler, the 1937-built 4-6-2 glides over the diamonds of the Connecticut River Line prior to backing to the engine terminal across the river in New Hampshire. Bill McChesney's skill at including railroad crew in his shots is apparent again in this portrayal of the fireman looking intently forward, garbed in the slightly soiled traditional dress of his profession.

(Above) Turning his gaze the other direction, the fire-man looks past the flanks of the tender as the engine makes its way past the station and toward the stone bridge over the Connecticut. The B&M applied the beautiful shaded red and gold lettering to a number of its steam engines in the 1940s, adding a welcome touch of elegance and color. One ball was the sign that the Rutland was cleared for the diamond; two for the Cheshire; and three for the Connecticut River mainline.

(Below) The 3716 safely out of the way, it's the Rutland's turn. Ten Wheeler 79 heads the FLYER over the diamonds west toward Rutland and a connection with the section coming from the New York Central connection at Troy over the Bennington line. Travelers on this section will glimpse some of the finest scenery in New England as the train passes over the Green Mountains, especially in the scenic area between Ludlow and Rutland, where the line heads upgrade through the Okemo National Forest to Mount Holly and downgrade through East Wallingford and the Clarendons before reaching Vermont's second city. Waiting in the background is an extra freight westbound, which will follow the passenger train out of Bellows Falls.

(Above) In a matter of minutes the freight appears, with another 4-6-0 flying the white flags of an extra. The Rutland crew and the crew of the B&M yard job share some thoughts before the 75 heads across the diamond and west to Rutland. The 1168 is an Alco S-1 switcher delivered to the road by Alco in 1944. The 75 also came from Alco, but in 1912, one of a group of six 4-6-0s delivered that year.

(Below) Waiting patiently for the westbounds to clear town is Mikado 32, in the hole at Riverside, just west of Bellows Falls, with another westbound by the waters of the Connecticut. The 32 was one of the six USRA light Mikados operated by the Rutland, built by Alco in 1918.

(Opposite page, top) Back at the diamonds the Central Vermont gets into the act as 2-10-4 706 bangs across the Rutland tracks with northbound freight 491. One of 10 Texas-type engines built by Alco in 1928, the CV 2-10-4s are the only ones of their type to operate in New England. Despite their Schenectady lineage they are pure CN in style, with characteristic Vanderbilt tender, tilted square emblem, and Elesco feedwater heaters atop the smokebox front. The 700s handled freights on the CV between Brattleboro, St. Albans and Montreal. Weight restrictions required that freights south of Brattleboro be handled by the CV's capable 2-8-0s. The CV's limited density usually saw only one freight train each way daily in daylight passing through Bellows Falls behind the 700s, so it was a treat to get the big fellow "bellowing" by on its way north.

(Opposite page, bottom) Passing by Bill and Pete we get a look at the hulking 706 from a different angle. Here its all-weather cab, CN-style Vanderbilt tender, and prolific plumbing accentuate its rugged looks. These 2-10-4s were minuscule compared to some of their type, in fact the smallest 2-10-4s built for an American railroad. But they were huge by New England standards. Low 60" drivers limited the hard-riding 700s to 35 miles per hour. The prominent trailing truck booster increased the tractive effort from just under 77,000 pounds to almost 90,000, letting them walk away with a yard full of freight. CV's rival Rutland had nothing to compare with the 700s, certainly not the little 4-6-0s Bill lensed earlier this glorious day, capable of only half the 706's rated power.

(Above) The final shot of this day finds Pete McChesney waving to the brakeman on the CV wooden van bringing up the rear of the northbound. Pete seems to be looking away from the train, perhaps a bit intimidated by the raw power of the big CV engine. The 491 left the New Haven connection at New London, CT in the early morning and will be in White River Junction by suppertime.

(Above) Bellows Falls usually provided a Rutland engine or two for the visiting rail photographer. Sprightly little 0-6-0 105 is steamed up and ready for service in the little Rutland yard just to the east of the Conn River diamonds. The 105 was a Schenectady product, class of 1913. She went to the scrapper in December 1951, part of the great purge of Rutland steam power as the road used the scrap value to buy new diesels.

(Below) Part of the first order of RS-3s received by the Rutland in 1951, the 204 rests between runs at Bellows Falls early in its tenure on the road, wearing the colors of its home state. Long after the Rutland vanished as a rail corporation, these colors will live on adorning the diesels of the Green Mountain Railroad, which operates the former road's Rutland-Bellows Falls line. We'll take a more detailed look at the Rutland a little later in this volume.

(Above) Bellows Falls was also a stop for B&M trains on the Connecticut River Line. On another sunny day the 4224 set is again on the lead of train 74 making its late afternoon stop at the station. Bellows Falls had about as many extra touches as any rail town in New England: ball signals, diamonds, various bridges, even a tunnel.

(Above) Farther up the Connecticut Valley lay another important rail town, White River Junction, VT. White River Junction, where the White River empties into the Connecticut, is the point at which the CV and B&M, which shared the Connecticut River trackage from East Northfield, MA, parted company, with the B&M continuing up the Connecticut to a connection with the Canadian Pacific at Wells River and to the White Mountains on its line to Berlin, NH, while the CV followed the White into the interior of Vermont on its route to St. Albans. The B&M's New Hampshire Mainline also made an appearance here, coming up from Boston and Concord, NH. Both the roads maintained engine facilities in this important location, the CV on the north side of White River Junction, the B&M across the river in New Hampshire. At White River, B&M's utilitarian 2-8-0 2716 poses on October 1, 1949. Unlike neighbors Rutland and Maine Central, the B&M didn't buy any new 2-8-2s, so its 2-8-0s assumed an important role as helpers, local freight engines, and occasional mainline haulers. The 2716 is a member of the last group of Consolidations purchased by the B&M from Brooks in 1916.

(Below) Texas type 708 was also at White River Junction on July 13, 1951. Given the assignments of the CV's big steam power, she will either head northwest for St. Albans, perhaps running through on the CN to Montreal, or take a trip south to Brattleboro along the Connecticut.

(Above) The 4-8-2 Mountain type was one of the most common and useful wheel arrangements for Eastern roads. The B&M, New Haven, New York Central, Rutland, and BAR all made use of the type in New England, as did the Central Vermont. CV's four 4-8-2s, 600-603, were most commonly used on passenger assignments, but also were no strangers to freight runs. Mountain 603 is waiting for its next assignment at the White River Junction engine terminal on July 13, 1951. She rolled out of Alco's Schenectady plant in 1927, part of the CV's late-1920s modernization program that saw the road acquire its only modern steam power, the U-1a 4-8-2s and the T-3a 2-10-4s delivered a year later.

(Left) As is often the case, the memorable and cloudless October 1, 1949 was followed by morning fog along the Connecticut. E-7 3813 splits the semaphores at Norwich, VT on October 2, 1949. The 3813 is one of 21 E-7s operated on the route of the Minute Man, joined in the fleet by a single E-8, 3821.

Central Vermont

CENTRAL VERMONT RAILWAY

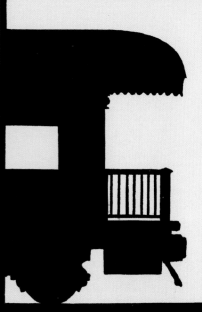

(Above) The last of the CV 2-8-0s, M-5a 475, heads northbound freight 491 past the southbound local at Stafford Springs, CT on October 22, 1949. This train is showing the usual practice of separating the two engines of a double-headed consist to account for weight restrictions on the numerous bridges dotting the CV's Southern Division.

The 325 mile Central Vermont during the late 19th century had dominated railroading in Vermont, but a series of financial crises had forced it to relinquish large parts of its system to rivals Rutland and Delaware & Hudson. Passing into the control of the Grand Trunk in 1898, it became a part of the Canadian National when the Canadian government created the CN system out of the Grand Trunk and other bankrupt roads in the early 1920s. It evolved into an important artery of the CN, giving it access to New England traffic on its line (shared since 1900 with the B&M) down the Connecticut River valley, and down to tidewater on its Southern Division between White River Junction, VT and New London, CT.

The CV operated its larger power, 2-10-4s and 4-8-2s, north of Brattleboro. The Southern Division trains south of Brattleboro relied on a fleet of capable 2-8-0s. We've seen the larger power; let's take a look at the Consolidations at work in the hills of Massachusetts and Connecticut.

(Left) In common with parent CN, CV was slow to dieselize its operations, continuing to field steam until early in 1957. Its 2-8-0s would become favorites of steam-starved railfans, but only those with hindsight would know that middle-aged 2-8-0s such as the 454 near Monson, MA with a southbound freight would write one of the final chapters of steam in New England, outlasted only by CP on its lines in Maine. When Bill shot the 1916 product on December 17, 1949, it was just another elderly steam engine hard at work at its usual duties, displaying the trademark McChesney smoke plume. The M-3a engines, 450-455, were a little older, slower, and less powerful than the M-5a 2-8-0s, numbered 460-475.

(Above and right) Once the northbound passes, we see the 454 again, distinguished from the 471 by the high-mounted Coffin feedwater heater on its smokebox. The CV 2-8-0s always seemed to convey a take-charge appearance that belied their middling size and strength.

(Left) Bill was back on the CV for a magnificent display of steam on June 10, 1950. At State Line, CT, the action starts with a double-headed northbound extra behind the 471 and the 466. The train has originated at New London as it heads into Massachusetts. Both engines are class M-5a, built by Alco in 1923, with 63" drivers and just under 50,000 pounds of tractive effort.

(Below) At Palmer, MA the northbound crosses the double tracks of the Boston & Albany after switching at the small yard just to the south of the diamonds. The B&A branch to Ware, now the Massachusetts Central, can be seen branching off to the right. At Brattleboro the 2-8-0s will hand off their train to one of the 2-10-4s for the trip north to the border.

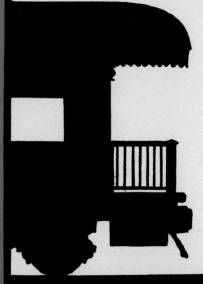

Hoosac Tunnel & Wilmington

A popular destination for New England railfan excursions in the pre-and postwar years was the little Hoosac Tunnel & Wilmington– the famous "Hoot, Toot & Whistle." This shortline accessed southern Vermont from a connection with the Boston & Maine at the east portal of Hoosac Tunnel, at the station of that name. It ran one of the first railfan excursions in 1934 and a half-dozen more before World War II put an end to such leisurely use of the nation's rail system. Bill was on hand for the trip on July 27, 1941, when over 600 passengers visited the remote little line along the Deerfield River.

(Above) The star attraction of the Hoot, Toot & Whistle was ancient 4-6-0 21. As this shot at Readsboro, VT, indicates, old number 21, built in 1892 for the Lake Shore & Michigan Southern, was no beauty; in fact, one might say she was so ugly she was almost cute, with her monstrous footboard pilot, high stack, and other generally mismatched style elements. She already had a half-century of service in when the revelers visited that last summer before the onslaught of war.

(Right) Before a series of floods devastated the line it had extended as far as Wilmington, VT, the largest community in this sparsely settled region (and known now as the location of the popular Mt. Snow ski area). In 1937 it was cut back to Readsboro, which was the "nerve center" and operating headquarters of the line. The 21 and a couple of the open-air cars used for excursions are inspected by railfans on the 1941 trip.

(Left) The other piece of equipment on the HT&W that captured the fancy of railfans was its double-ended snowplow, a very useful piece of equipment in the snowy hills of southern Vermont and northern Massachusetts.

(Below) Could that be Lucius Beebe himself in the straw boater? The railfan excursions of the prewar era were immensely popular. What could have been better than a relaxed trip in the clean air of the Berkshires, pulled by an engine right out of the previous century?

Boston & Albany

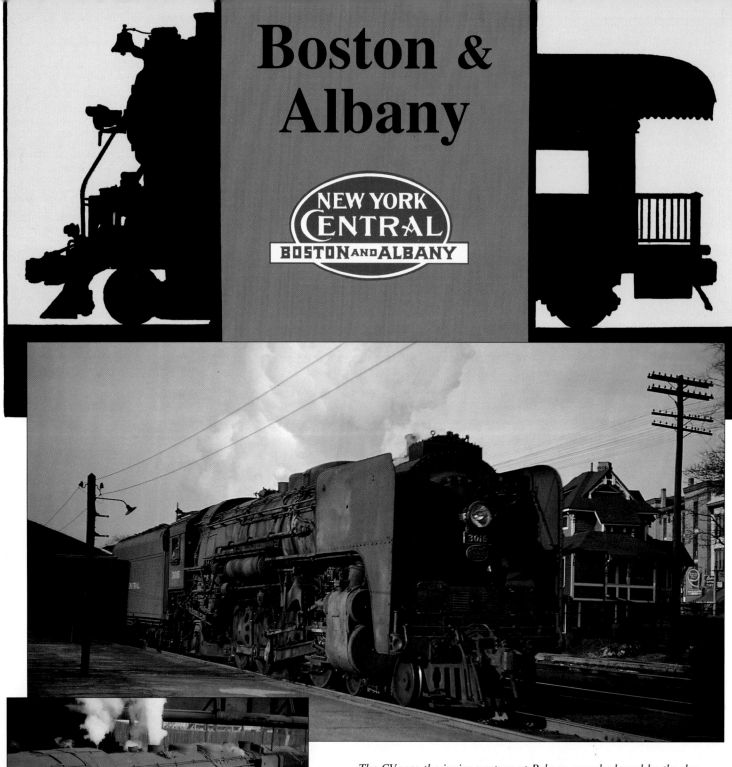

NEW YORK
Central
BOSTON AND ALBANY

The CV was the junior partner at Palmer, overshadowed by the double-tracked main of the Boston & Albany, the New York Central's artery through Massachusetts to Boston's South Station. B&A obtained 20 J-2 Hudsons for passenger service on the hilly B&A route, numbered 600-620. They were virtually identical to the Central's J-1 machines, but had smaller drivers, a curious square sand dome, and stubby tenders.

(Above) The B&A was Central's mountain railroad, and the bigger passenger trains of the late 1930s and 1940s taxed the 4-6-4s to the limits. The Central system was coming back from the Depression and needed to address the need for more modern power systemwide. The answer given in 1940 was the L-3 Mohawk, a virtual Hudson look-alike but with more guts. The first 25, built by Alco and numbered 3000-3024, were designed to be dual-service engines with passenger pilots. On December 17, 1949, L-3a 4-8-2 3016 has train 22, the eastbound LAKE SHORE LIMITED easing into Palmer around 1 PM. The smoke lifters were added after production to enhance crew visibility.

(Above) Once again Bill has his marvelous touch for capturing not just the engines but the men who operate them. The engineer of the Mohawk whistles off from the brief stop at Palmer. We can be assured that the "resume speed" sign will be honored as the train runs off the final miles on the long trek from Lake Michigan to Massachusetts Bay.

Rutland

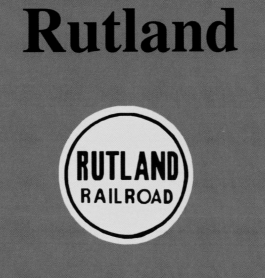
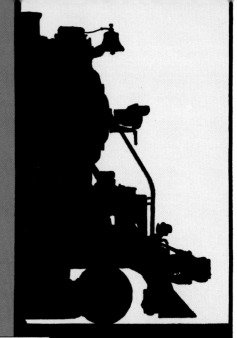

(*Left*) Bill captures the look and feel of the Rutland with this charcoal drawing of a steam engine proceeding west out of the Connecticut River Valley toward the Green Mountains looming in the background. The characteristic diagonal braces on the telegraph poles and the patterning of the locomotive running board are indications of Bill's attention to detail in his artwork.

Pity the Rutland. If ever a railroad had the odds stacked against it, this 407 mile carrier (in 1950) in New York and Vermont did. Vermont was typical of Northern New England rail redundancy. In a state with the smallest population in the East, there were in 1950 over 900 miles of mainline trackage, more than in populous and industrialized Connecticut and over half the total in Massachusetts, with a population over 10 times greater than the Green Mountain state. Vermont was 50% above the national average in miles of railroad per capita, even 20% above the average of railroad miles per square mile of area. This led to anemic figures for rail revenues, which for Vermont roads averaged only 1/3 the national average per rail mile.

The Rutland was well-named, for the namesake city was the key to the operations of the road. Here, in west central Vermont, lines headed north to Burlington and a connection at Ogdensburg, NY with the New York Central; east to the B&M connection at Bellows Falls; and south to Bennington, where until 1953 trains continued on to Chatham, NY and a B&A connection. At North Bennington the road connected with the B&M's branch to the Mechanicville mainline at Hoosick Junction, NY.

The Rutland competed head to head with the Delaware & Hudson, with a more direct route from the Canadian border to New York State; with the Central Vermont, part of the Canadian National family of roads; and the Canadian Pacific, which could penetrate New England by its lines to Vermont and connections with the B&M and Maine Central. The Rutland was historically associated with the New York Central, but the bigger carrier had lost interest in the little road during the Depression and, along with the New Haven, which also held Rutland stock, had liquidated its interests in the Rutland in 1941.

Serving no city larger than Burlington, with a 1950 population around 30,000, and ending in locations barely identifiable to those not schooled in geography, the Rutland managed nonetheless to reorganize as the Rutland Railway in 1950 and begin a belated modernization program. Under the leadership of Gardner Caverly, a Vermont businessman, the 1950s were years of remarkable prosperity (even paying a dividend in certain years) before the calamitous strike of 1961 put an end to the road. Passenger service ended in 1953, the payroll was trimmed, and unprofitable branches torn up and sold for scrap.

75

Bill and Pete visited the Rutland several times before the end of steam. In this August 21, 1949 scene, the yard and engine terminal at Rutland is all steam, as two switchers and a 2-8-0 cluster around the smoke-stained coaling tower. It will be two years before diesels begin sullying the steam scene at Rutland.

(Left) Earlier in 1949, February 24 to be exact, three year old 4-8-2 92 heads a northbound double-headed freight up the line at Manchester. The four modern 4-8-2s were the best of Rutland's steam fleet, equally at home on freight and passenger assignments.

(Right) Until the discontinuance of passenger service after the 1953 strike, the Rutland tried mightily to compete for the dwindling numbers of passengers in its lightly populated service area. With the D&H, CV, and B&M all contesting for the passenger trade between Canada and New York and New England, it's a testament to the determination of the Rutland that it maintained its service as along as it did. In this scene of New England railroading at its best, Pacific 84 has the GREEN MOUNTAIN FLYER northbound at Middlebury late in the afternoon of August 21, 1949, heading up the verdant Champlain Valley toward Burlington and the border. Hopefully for the passengers, it isn't too hot this afternoon, for the Rutland never owned any air-conditioned equipment.

(Above) The year of change for the Rutland was 1951, when this bastion of steam began a quick transition to a road powered almost entirely by Alco road switchers. Fortunately, Bill was on hand for a remarkable final swan song of steam on the Rutland that year, beginning with a three-way meet at East Dorset, VT, about halfway between Rutland and Bennington. Mikado 36 sits in the hole with a southbound freight, waiting for both the northbound and southbound GREEN MOUNTAIN FLYERS to pass. The 36 is running out the string, and will be retired before the end of the year.

(Left) First to appear is the northbound section, with Pacific 81 in charge of four cars. This is the Troy section of the train, which will be combined at Rutland with the Boston section for the trip to the St. Lawrence. The train began its trip northward over the B&M's Troy Branch to Johnsonville, NY, where it met the Fitchburg mainline for the run to Hoosick Junction, NY. From there it diverged onto the branch to North Bennington, VT, where it met the Rutland's Bennington-Rutland mainline.

(Above) The northbound squeezes into the siding and noses up to the 2-8-2, leaving room for the southbound section to pass on the main. The area between East Dorset and Manchester Center to the south was an excellent place to frame shots of the Rutland, as it passed through marshes framed on both sides by the ridges of the Green Mountains.

(Below) Here comes the southbound FLYER, led by the 92, one of the four modern L-1 4-8-2s purchased from Alco in 1946. These handsome light Mountains were the last 4-8-2s constructed for an American railroad. Delivered in a green and yellow scheme, the "Green Hornets" by 1951 are wearing black, but still present a pretty picture of light but state-of-the-art power appropriate to the needs of the Rutland. The higher elevations in the background are covered in snow, but it's nonetheless rare to see bare ground in Vermont in February.

(All) As the southbound continues on its way to Troy, where it will connect with the New York Central for travelers continuing on to Albany and New York, the northbound backs out of the passing track onto the main. Pacific 81 was one of six 4-6-2s on the Rutland, built by Alco in 1925 along with the 80 and 82; the 83-85 joined them in 1929. The 80-82 were low-drivered by 4-6-2 standards, at 69", but then again the Rutland was not exactly a speedway.

(Above) Both passenger trains gone, it's now the turn of the freight to continue its trip southward to Bennington, where it will make connections with the B&M. At this time, it is still possible that some of the freight cars will make their way down the Corkscrew Division to the B&A connection at Chatham, NY, which is in its final two years of operation. At Manchester, the snow covered mass of Mt. Equinox, the second highest mountain in Vermont, forms the background for the passing southbound.

(Below) The Rutland rostered 17 2-8-0s in the postwar years, built between 1907 and 1913. New England railroads seemed to roster a large number of engines built between 1905-1920 that just lasted and lasted until eventual replacement by diesels. The 26, seen at Rutland in 1951, is a transitional engine with modern piston cylinders but old-style Stephenson valve gear. It is one of six members of class G-34d, numbered 26-31, and will go to the scrapper at the end of 1951.

(Above) Rutland was the best spot on the system to find a variety of the road's 58 steam engines in the waning years of steam operations. On September 22, 1951, Mountain 93 reposes at the engine terminal. Note that 93 has lettering on her tender, unlike the 81 and 92 seen in the meet at East Dorset. The four L-1s could have lasted well into the 1950s had the decision not be made around 1950 to go with diesels.

(Below) Also at Rutland that sunny day was Ten Wheeler 74. Built at Schenectady the year before the 26, the 4-6-0 has a modern appearance due to the utilization of Walschaerts valve gear along with nonslanted piston cylinders. All 10 of the Rutland's "modern" 4-6-0s had 69" drivers, making them ideal for dual service work. The striping on the running boards is a nice touch.

(Above) September 30, 1951 was the date of the annual Exchange Club special from Chatham, NY to Rutland and return. These trips were popular, usually running over 10 cars. The 1951 trip was the last under steam; in fact, steam had been eliminated on the line from Bennington to Chatham earlier that year, and the trip, powered by Mountain 93, had to be run as later steam trips were, with special arrangements to keep it watered and coaled on the trip down the Corkscrew. The lengthy train is seen heading north toward Rutland in a shot taken from the caboose trailing the wooden passenger equipment.

(Above) The Gay Nineties was the theme of the day at Rutland.

(Right) An unusual tender-first view of the 93 shows off her lean and clean lines. The gold number on the back of the tender is an unusual placement that modelers might miss in most pictures. Like most Rutland steam engines, the 4-8-2s were built at Schenectady to designs based on New York Central prototypes. Along with Pacifics 83-85, the Mountains were the only Rutland steamers with 73" drivers, making them the speediest as well as the most powerful engines in the Rutland arsenal.

(Above) The theme of the trip was the Gay Nineties, and fancy outfits and bunting were the rule of the day. The 93 was the last steam engine built for the Rutland, in 1946. One of her crew oils her rods while some of the excursioners take a close look at RS-3 202, one of the new diesels that have vanquished her and the other Rutland steamers.

(Below) The riders on that year's Exchange Club excursion were able to see Rutland bustling with steam activity in the eleventh hour of steam locomotion on the Green Mountain Route. Diesels were arriving from Alco throughout the second half of 1951 and into 1952, spelling the end of steam on the road. Fortunately for the McChesneys and others that day steam was still in charge of most of the operations. Pacific 82 is in charge of the northbound FLYER at the Rutland passenger station downtown, about to head north to Burlington. The proud train has only another year and a half of existence until it and all Rutland passenger service ends in 1953.

(Above) Ten Wheeler 76 arrives in Rutland from Bellows Falls with the meagre two-car Boston section of the FLYER. The sun returns to highlight the lines of the 4-6-0 as it backs out of the station area and switches tracks before proceeding to the engine terminal. The Howe Scale Company, located between the Bellows Falls and Bennington lines, was a landmark familiar to generations of travelers on the Rutland.

(Below) A highlight of the trip that September day was a visit to the Rutland's engine shops. Pacific type 85 is in a state of considerable disarray in the shop bay. Steam engines were low-down and dirty when their innards were revealed, much like old teakettles after years of boiling hard water. This engine was the newest of the 4-6-2s and the last to be retired, early in 1953.

(Above) Also in the shops was 4-6-2 81, looking spic-and-span after its servicing, belying the short time it has left to serve the Rutland.

(Left) Outside the shops was Ten Wheeler 71, a 1910 product of Alco whose active service life is coming to an end. One of four class F-2-h 4-6-0s, its classification was changed to F-2-k when it was modernized with Walschaerts valve gear in 1917.

(Right) Pete poses in the cab in classic steam attire. The 71's double cab windows are a giveaway of the influence that the New York Central exerted on the Vermont carrier in the first decades of the twentieth century. Inside the cab we see the firebox doors and controls of the venerable locomotive, already beginning to rust like the smokebox door.

The future of the Rutland appears in the form of Alco RS-3 202, one of nine of the 1600 horsepower road switchers that appeared in 1951-52 to dieselize the road, along with a single GE 70 ton unit and five RS-1s. The RS-3s were true dual-purpose engines, equally at home on freight, milk, and passenger assignments on the Rutland. Like its neighbor D&H across Lake Champlain, the Rutland found in the RS-3 the answer to its motive power needs. In its first few months of operation, the 202 heads the Bellows Falls/Boston section of the FLYER past the ball signals in downtown Rutland for the scenic 52 mile trip to the Connecticut River and connection with the B&M's Cheshire Branch.

(Below) The Troy section of the FLYER that milky September day heads out under the command of B&M P-3 class Pacific 3704. One of 10 of her class built by Alco in 1923, she is working off the mileage necessitated by the routing of the train over the B&M between North Bennington and Troy. At this time, the Pacifics assigned to this service were captives on the west end of the B&M. Elimination of the electrification through Hoosac Tunnel in the late 1940s dieselized operations west of Greenfield and east of Mechanicville and Troy with the exception of the Rutland pool trains.

(*Above*) Accelerating out of the station, the 3704 heads to the right and the Bennington line; the line to Bellows Falls is visible in the background.

(*Below*) Our final shot of the Rutland is a Bill McChesney special: the fireman of Ten Wheeler 79 leans out his cab window, a thoughtful expression on his face. Perhaps he has a glimmer of the future, the good years of the 1950s quickly erased by the troubles that in a decade will spell the end of this proud Vermont railroad.

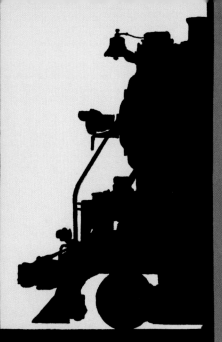

Quebec Railway Light and Power Company

Let's take a sidetrip to the territory just north of the Rutland, the Province of Quebec, for a look at the unusual electric railway operations along the St. Lawrence from Quebec City to St. Joachim, along the north shore of the St. Lawrence River. The Quebec Railway, as it was known, was really two operations under one company, an urban street railway system serving the city and the line up the river. The latter served two important tourist locations, Montmorency Falls and the shrine of St. Anne de Beaupre. It also provided the Canadian National entree to the city from its Murray Bay Subdivision further north along the river. In the postwar years, the electric company lost interest in its railway, eliminating the urban Citadel division in favor of buses in 1948. It sold the line to St. Joachim to CN for $750,000 in 1951; included in the deal were nine electric trolley cars, seven steeple-cab electric locomotives, even a steam engine for use when the power went out! In 1957 the CN pulled down the wires but continued to operate passenger and freight trains over the historic little line, using Budd cars to replace the Ottawa Car Manufacturing motor cars.

(Right) Relettered for its new owner, electric motor 226 poses at the company's shops in February 1953. No, it was not Quebec Railway practice to run a tender behind their electrics!

(Above) The CN needed the 25 mile Quebec Railway line to allow its trains from Clermont to reach Quebec City, 92.1 miles away. In February, 1953 it's business as usual as engine 35, one of the larger units and still lettered for the Quebec Railway, heads train 176 north to Clermont through the back streets of Quebec. This was one of two daily passenger runs on the line each way to connect with the CN, a service that predated acquisition of the line by the big trunk road.

(Above) The scenic highlight of the line was Montmorency Falls, which cascade 274 feet down a rugged hillside about a 20 minute ride north of Quebec. Wooden car 405 was one of three wooden cars left at the time of the CN takeover; it dated from the 1880s. This was an abbreviated train; usually the motor cars pulled trailers of either closed or open vestibule design. In 1953, when all these shots were taken, the operation still saw 24 trains operated daily.

(Left) Pete poses with an ancient wooden boxcar equipped with Fox trucks, used by the road for storage and work service.

Delaware & Hudson

The venerable Delaware & Hudson was a pioneering transportation company in America. Beginning as a canal company in the 1820s hauling hard coal north from the Pennsylvania anthracite fields to markets along the Hudson River, it quickly embraced the new railroad technology and became a major regional line, hauling coal to markets in New York, New England, and Canada, passengers between New York City and Montreal through a partnership with the New York Central, and bridge line traffic between western points and a connection with the Boston & Maine at the sprawling Mechanicville, NY yard. The D&H enjoyed decades of prosperity under the quixotic leadership of Leonor F. Loree, the "emperor of the D&H" who favored slow and powerful hand-fired 2-8-0s, English-styled Pacifics, and autocratic management style. The imperious Loree was gone by 1938, replaced by Joseph H. Nuelle, who had led the NYO&W and later the L&NE. Nuelle's experience at the smaller anthracite roads during the dark years of the Great Depression no doubt taught him to take noth-

ing for granted, and he launched a period of innovation and modernization that astounded observers accustomed to Loree's conservatism. The hallmarks of the Nuelle period, which lasted from 1938 to 1954, were the big and modern Challengers and Northerns that rolled off the assembly line at the Alco plant at Schenectady, hard by the D&H mainline. Early dieselization with a fleet of somber black Alco road switchers spelled the end of the modern steam era on the D&H by the early 1950s, but Bill McChesney was able to memorialize in color the D&H's finest in steam on one of the most photogenic and beautiful railroads in the East. Bill found his way to the Champlain Division, stretching north along Lake Champlain from Whitehall, NY to Canada, and the Susquehanna Division, linking the Capital District area of New York with Oneonta and Binghamton. Steam was making its last stand on the Delaware & Hudson, and we are fortunate that Bill was able to track down the fast-disappearing steam locomotives on the Bridge Line.

(Left) The northbound LAURENTIAN pauses at the Whitehall, NY station in February 1953, showing off a somewhat grimy round-end observation car displaying the train's name. The train is a joint venture of the D&H and New York Central between the largest cities of Canada and the U. S., with the D&H exchanging responsibilities with the Central at Troy. Whitehall is at the southern end of Lake Champlain; the passengers on the train this snowless winter day have the spectacular vistas alongside the lake to look forward to in the next hours.

(Below) Shooting through the windows of the observation car, Bill lensed the station at Westport as the train resumed its northward trek after making the station stop. Westport is 63 miles south of Rouses Point, a spectacular point at which the mountains crowd in on a wide bay of the lake. The station has the distinctive cupola favored by the D&H.

(Left) On August 21, 1949, K class Northern 302 heads the southbound LAURENTIAN into Ticonderoga, NY. The Alco-built 4-8-4 is one of 15 dual service delivered in 1943, during the peak traffic years of World War II. Assigned primarily to Albany-Montreal passenger trains and freights north of Oneonta, the 75"-drivered Northerns complemented the road's 4-6-6-4 Challengers. Together the two types epitomized the change of philosophy as D&H modernized its steam motive power fleet in the 1940s. The 302 would make the last steam passenger run on the D&H just four years later, on July 17, 1953.

(*Above*) The 312 rests at the CP's Glenn Engine Terminal in Montreal on September 1, 1951, awaiting a return to the States with a southbound passenger, either the daytime LAURENTIAN or the overnight MONTREAL LIMITED. The 312 combines the modern Alco look with some traces of earlier D&H style, including the lighted side numberboards and smoke lifters. The D&H utilized trackage and facilities of the Canadian Pacific in the Montreal area, as evidenced by the CP roadswitcher in the background.

(*Above*) Peering out of the gloom of Windsor Station's trainshed is D&H Pacific 603. Built by Alco in 1914, she has been extensively modified to give her the modern D&H look: boiler jacketing, recessed headlight, smoke lifters, capped stack. She is one of ten 4-6-2s on the D&H, usually assigned to the road's premier Montreal-Albany trains. At this late date, September 1, 1951, she is sharing these duties with the 4-8-4s and the new RS-3s that will send her to scrap in 1952.

(Right) E-5a 2-8-0 1113 shows off its unique lines at Fort Edward, NY on August 21, 1949. Only the D&H under Leonor Loree could have produced this beast, with its tiny cab perched perilously on the bulging Wootten firebox, triple domes, smallish tender, and enormous boiler. Built in 1927, the same year neighboring New York Central began acquiring its 4-6-4s, the 1113 is pure 1920s drag era power, built to lug millions of tons of Pennsylvania anthracite north to markets in New York, New England, and Canada. Fort Edward is the junction of the Albany-Montreal mainline and the Lake George Branch, and waiting in the background is another 2-8-0, camelback 819, assigned to the branch. It's hard to believe these totally dissimilar engines share the same wheel arrangement.

(Above) At Lake George Village, NY, the 819 rests at the Italianate station preparatory to the southbound run down the branch to Fort Edward. Prospect Mountain forms the background for the little 819 at the popular resort town. Close to the water's edge, the station afforded travelers the opportunity to board one of the steamers plying the waters of pristine Lake George, the southernmost and perhaps most beautiful lakes in the Adirondack Mountains.

(Right) The sun glints off the firebox of the 819 as it rounds the wye at Lake George. Not too many camelback 2-8-0s were hauling passenger trains on Class I railroads in 1949! The passenger service to Lake George by this date was summer only. It's August 21, 1949, and soon autumn will start making its presence known in this northern region. The E-3a class 819, a 1906 product of Alco's Dunkirk Works, has another two years of life before making the trip to Luria Brothers scrapyard in the D&H's great purge of steam power in 1951.

(Right) Sometimes the greatest railroad photographs are the simplest, where subject, lighting, and setting combine to create a classic scene. Such is the case with D&H 4-6-6-4 1511, beginning its descent of Howe Cave Hill on D&H's Susquehanna Division on October 29, 1949 with a northbound hotshot freight bound for the B&M interchange at Mechanicville. The engineer and Pete McChesney exchange waves on this warm late autumn day in New York's Schoharie Valley. The D&H's 35 Challengers were received from on-line builder American Locomotive Company's Schenectady plant just before World War II, as new president Joseph H. Nuelle transformed the road from a coal carrier employing drag era 2-8-0s to a bridge line specializing in fast freight movements. Their reign on the D&H lasted barely a decade before a huge fleet of black RS-3s transformed the road's motive power fleet once again.

(Below) As the train glides by, we get a chance to examine the compact lines of the 1511 accented by the gold striping around the cab. In the hillside in the background is the entrance to Howe Caverns, a popular tourist attraction in this part of New York State. In the immediate background is one of many quarries in this mineral-rich region.

(Above) A few miles to the west that late October day in 1949, the image of the D&H past is seen in the form of E-5a 2-8-0 1114 at the station at Cobleskill. The D&H in the years under the presidency of the formidable Leonor F. Loree had stuck with low-drivered drag era 2-8-0s as it primary freight power throughout the 1920s and 1930s. The apotheosis of the 2-8-0 on the road was the E-5a, 12 of which were built at the road's Colonie Shops outside Albany between 1926 and 1930. The 1114 is at the head of a southbound about to put the 71,000 pounds of tractive effort to the ultimate test of Richmondville Hill, the ruling southbound grade on the line. This engine once wore a semi-streamlined boiler jacket and skyline casting atop the boiler, but sacrificed these to the war effort.

(Below) The end of a great day of rail photography: Bill's Leica captures the splendor of the New York Central's Water Level Route as a Niagara heads eastbound along the Mohawk River east of Amsterdam, NY with a good-sized train. The low sun angle highlights the 80" drivers and clean modern lines of the 4-8-4. We'll see more of the Niagaras and the passenger trains of the New York Central in the next chapter as we continue our journey south to the banks of the Hudson River.

New York Central

NEW YORK CENTRAL SYSTEM

(Above) On September 3, 1949, Bill positioned himself atop a rock cut at Roa Hook just north of the Peekskill station to shoot the armada of passenger trains leaving New York westbound in the late afternoon. The light is just a bit backlit and low-angled, highlighting the running gear and smooth, powerful lines of one of the Central's finest, Niagara 6000, on the move towards Albany and points west. This is the first of 27 Niagaras, delivered in 1945-46.

By 1949, when Bill McChesney began his photographic coverage of the New York Central, the lordly road of the Vanderbilts was in serious trouble. Traditionally the number two railroad in America behind its archrival Pennsylvania (which was actually a bit smaller in mileage), the Central epitomized all the problems beginning to afflict railroads in the postwar period, especially those in the East. The NYC had always been committed to the finest passenger service in the East, in the Vanderbilt tradition utilizing the finest stations, engines, equipment, and providing service second to none. It operated a substantial commuter passenger service on several lines heading north from New York City along both sides of the Hudson and into the hills of Westchester and Putnam counties in New York. It was heavily reliant upon the older manufacturing industries in its home state and in the industrialized states of the Midwest. It had a huge investment in its physical plant and rolling stock, both of which reflected a traditional 50/50 split between freight and passenger operations. But five years after the end of the war, only 25% of the road's revenues were coming from its extensive passenger operations. The worst was on the horizon: building of the New York State Thruway in the mid-1950s would cut even more deeply into its passenger operations; trucks took aim on the high-tariff goods such as meat, fruit, and machinery that the Central relied upon.

The Central was also curiously passive in the merger planning allowed by the Transportation Act of 1940. Unlike rival Pennsy, which was constantly investing in the stocks and bonds of railroads likely to play a part in the shuffling of systems in the East, the Central only dabbled inconclusively, talking with the Lackawanna which, increasingly bereft of the anthracite revenues that made it rich, made little sense as a partner. A 1948 bid by Robert Young of C&O to sit on the Central's Board was rebuffed.

Internally, the Central recognized rather late the need to dieselize. The big years for equipment purchases were 1949-1951, when over

(Above) That same afternoon at track level Bill lensed Hudson 5307 heading north with a local. The 5307 is one of 275 members of the Central's fleet of 4-6-4s. First delivered to the road in 1927, they instantly captured the fancy of the industry and the public, which regarded them as perhaps the most beautiful and successful passenger steam engines of all time.

$225 million was spent to modernize the big trunk line. These were the years that Bill McChesney afforded us a look at the New York Central in a time of transition. His favorite territory was the Hudson River Valley north of Gotham, along the east bank of the river. This was the fabled "Water Level Route," a four-track avenue heading north from the metropolis to Albany and points west. Electrified as far as Harmon, 32 miles north of Grand Central Station, the line hugged the east bank of the river through scenery described by travelers as the finest in the East. During these years, the fleet of intercity expresses was joined by numerous freights serving the industries of Yonkers and Tarrytown as well as New York City itself, served by the West Side Yard in Manhattan. In addition, there were frequent commuter trains to Harmon and on up the line to Poughkeepsie; milk trains; mail and express; and locals terminating at Albany, 140 miles north of the Big Apple.

For the railfan, it was a glorious fin-de-siecle spectacle of New York Central operations in the grand manner. In 1954 Robert Young and his operations lieutenant, Alfred Perlman, finally gained power over the Central. They found a railroad that badly needed modernizing, and began in the time-honored fashion by paring passenger service, cutting back on the physical plant, and begging for relief from commuter operations. By 1958, the Central's woes were critical; Young committed suicide; and the first steps were taken toward consummating railroad's ultimate tragi-comic folly, the Penn Central merger.

(Right) In June of 1950 Bill rode a special from New Haven over the Maybrook Line to Hopewell Junction, NY and down the 13 mile branch to Beacon, on the east bank of the Hudson. The two DL-109s make a fine sight alongside the New York Central's Hudson Division mainline. The excursioners are looking forward to a glimpse of the nonstop action on the busy New York Central.

(Above) Here comes the tonnage! Mohawk type 3124 heads a seemingly endless train of 40' boxcars up the valley through Beacon, treating the railfans who've come into town on the New Haven special with a display of big-time railroading in the traditional manner. The 4-8-2 was the favored type of freight engine on the NYC from 1916 until dieselization: 600 engines of this wheel arrangement at one time or another served the system. In the background loom the Hudson Highlands, the extension of the Blue Ridge that the Hudson cuts through between Peekskill and Beacon.

(Below) Blasting through the old river town the modern L-4 4-8-2 shows off its special features: the Scullin disk drivers, smoke lifters, and large tender with a huge 43 ton coal capacity. Once again, Bill seems to have the special knack of making his pictures come alive by the prominence of crew members, even on moving trains like this one. We can be sure that for steam fans who had to suffer the indignity of riding into town on a diesel – albeit a DL-109 set – this made their day.

(Above) Earlier that spring, another trip to Beacon yielded this shot of a northbound workaday local behind J-1 Hudson 5240. Before the building of the Newburgh-Beacon bridge (now I-84) Beacon offered ferry service to its sister city on the West Shore from the vicinity of the train station. The river town is 58 miles north of New York City.

(Below) The Mohawks were somewhat overshadowed by the more glamorous Hudsons and the newer, superpower Niagaras. But from the introduction in 1916 of the L-1s, and especially after the modern high horsepower L-3s and L-4s arrived, the 4-8-2s were the key to freight operations on the main lines of the New York Central. Like the B&O and Pennsy, the NYC found the 4-8-2 the perfect type of large modern steam freight power to meet its needs. The type was also able to handle passenger assignments, as seen here with the 3138 heading up the valley at Breakneck Ridge with a northbound standard train. In this section of the valley the river cuts through the mountain ridge, requiring a number of tunnels on the Hudson Division and the parallel West Shore line barely visible in the background of this shot, hugging the river bank just north of West Point.

(Above) Just to the south Mohawk L-4 3123 is about to enter the tunnel at Breakneck Mountain with a northbound freight. The date is July 1, 1950. In these years just after the war, the freight business to New York City was still booming, before trucks siphoned it off. Who would have believed that far-off summer evening that less than half a century later there would be no freight service to Manhattan, and the 30th Street Yard on the west side of Manhattan would be abandoned and empty?

(Below) Later that evening, one of the Central's penultimate Hudsons, J-3a class 5409, shows off her stuff with another of the endless string of passenger trains that still graced the Hudson Valley in 1950. Note the Boston & Albany lettered combine just behind the tender. The McChesneys favored this scenic stretch of the Hudson, and often camped out on one of the islands nearby on their visits to the area.

(Above) July 1, 1950 was also a day of some unusual assignments for Central 4-6-4s. In a bizarre move, Hudson 5216 is running tender-first along the water's edge toward Harmon with a Poughkeepsie local passenger run.

(*Above*) The prize catch that busy afternoon was J-3a Hudson 5405 exiting the tunnel at Breakneck Mountain with a freight bound for the West Side Line in Manhattan. The speedy Hudsons, with their 79" drivers, seemed improbable dual-purpose engines, but in the final years of steam were sometimes found on trains like this. We can be sure that those vintage boxcars are getting a fast run down the engine's namesake valley.

(*Left*) Milk was a commodity that left the railroads earlier than most. By 1950, when Hudson 5306 was caught barreling north with a train of empty milk cars from New York City, milk accounted for only about $7 million in annual revenues for all roads combined. As a perishable commodity requiring dedicated equipment, fast schedules, and considerable terminal expenses, milk traffic was expendable for trunk roads like the Central, but still a necessity for smaller lines like the Rutland to maintain for survival.

(Opposite page, top) The curve at Roa Hook, just north of Peekskill, provides the setting for this portrait of L-2a Mohawk 2746 heading south for Harmon on August 29, 1949. At Harmon it will head for the engine terminal and an electric locomotive will continue the trip down the West Side Line to the busy 30th Street Yard.

(Opposite page, bottom) Looking north at Roa Hook, Hudson 5220 provides us this tender-first going-away angle of New York Central's most famous engine. In the distance the black rock of one of the numerous cuts along the Hudson Division reminds us how difficult it was to create this multi-track speedway in the rugged section between Peekskill and Beacon.

(Above) A closer view of a Mohawk: the 3042 heads a northbound train of empties returning from Gotham, at Peekskill, 41 miles up the line. This engine has a rather unique front-end treatment, with a footboard pilot, smokelifters, Elesco feedwater, and extended smokebox. It is a member of class L-3b, built by Lima in 1940 for fast freight service. Check out those company stock cars trailing the Mohawk, probably headed out west for another load of cattle.

(Above) Another of the handsome K-3 Pacifics, the 4739, heads a Poughkeepsie local north at Peekskill, NY, with the river just visible to the right. Note the unusual amber-over-amber signal indication on this stretch of double track. It's September 3, 1949.

(Right) Back on the rock cut above Peekskill, Bill turns his attention to the north, where Hudson 5405 is seen again, this time approaching with a southbound local. The Peekskill area has long been a favorite of photographers shooting the line up the east bank of the river. As this shot shows, it's a good place to get on the west side of the tracks, a necessity for good afternoon lighting, and still show the river.

(Left) At the Peekskill station on September 3, 1949, L-4 Mohawk 3106 trundles north with another train of high cars, including several Pacemaker boxcars. The smoke-lifters are doing an admirable job of keeping the soft-coal smoke out of the eyes of the engine crew, allowing the fireman to fix his attention to the man with a Leica commemorating the passage of his train on its trip to Selkirk Yard near Albany, and points west. The passenger pilot on this engine reveals its dual-service role on the Central, although freight was the primary role of the Mohawks by 1949, with diesel passenger engines already on board and more to come.

(Left) Later that afternoon, the 4667 makes an appearance with another northbound local near Peekskill. Peekskill was noted in the postwar years as the spot on the widening Hudson where many of the nation's fleet of World War II Liberty Ships sat idly at anchor for years, waiting for buyers or an upturn in the fortunes of the American merchant marine that never eventuated.

(Right) Its earlier run to Poughkeepsie long completed, the 4739 comes smoking by Bill's rocky vantage point running light back to Harmon. Surely the dispatcher could not be too happy with this non-revenue movement at the double-track pinchpoint in the four-track route, right in the middle of the commuter and passenger rush late in the day.

Looking north at Roa Hook, a northbound passenger train heads through the small Anthony's Nose Tunnel.

(Above) Mohawk 2785 bursts out of the southbound bore of the tunnel at Breakneck with a southbound freight. The Mohawks in class L-2a delivered in 1925 predated the Hudsons; looks-wise they resembled the 2-8-2s that preceded them as the Central's mainline power, with the Elesco feedwater heater slung prominently over the smokebox.

(Below) In the early days of color photography, the short days of winter meant taking a chance that show film and lenses could still freeze a fast-moving train. On the short afternoon of January 15, 1949, Bill took a chance that he could still shoot this northbound express behind an A-B set of E-7s led by the 4017. The low light picks up the lightning striping of the classic units nicely as the trains rounds the big bend at Cold Spring, NY.

(Above) Laying down a beautiful plume of steam on the cold afternoon, a K-3 Pacific heads north into the bores at Breakneck.

(Left) Pushing his equipment even closer to its limits, Bill stood between the eastbound and westbound tracks at the foot of the Breakneck tunnels to record a J-3 Hudson at speed — probably around 85 miles per hour — wheel by a slower northbound freight with a milk train.

To keep traffic moving along the busy mainline the Central relied on track pans to enable steam locomotives to pick up water on the fly. The system also enabled the road to equip its steamers with tenders having a greater coal capacity, extending their fuel range. On a road with a northern climate such as the NYC, the pans had to be kept thawed by heating plants located adjacent to the facility. Bill took a look at the Central's operations at Clinton Point on the Hudson south of Poughkeepsie in March of 1949, when dieselization of the vast New York Central system was still less than 25% complete.

(Above) Its nose blurred by the speed of its passage, one of Central's massive 6000-series Niagaras barrels past, the white of its steam plume matching the spray cascading around the bottom of the tender as it rewaters itself for the final miles of its trip to Harmon with a southbound passenger train. Bill has to be careful–it's not too pleasant to be sprayed with freezing water from a speeding 4-8-4, and not too good for cameras, either.

(Below) Next along is one of the L-4b Mohawks, the 3163, heading a long train of boxcars and reefers north. The 25 members of this group of 4-8-2s were equipped with scoops to allow them to take water on the fly.

(Above and below) Pacific 4675 hits the pans northbound with a local passenger consist. In the foreground we can see the aftereffects of the Niagara's passage. The going away shot illustrates some of the support facilities needed to keep the operation going on cold days like this one.

Not all the New York Central's operations north of New York City were confined to the Water Level Route. In the hills of that part of New York State that lies east of the Hudson the Central operated two other north-south lines that provided commuters in the affluent Westchester and Putnam County suburbs access to New York by rail. The Harlem Division extended 105 miles from New York to Chatham, NY, where it connected with the Boston & Albany main. The Putnam Division extended into its namesake county from High Bridge in New York to a connection with the Harlem Division at Putnam Junction just outside Brewster, NY, 51.9 miles north of New York City. Both lines roughly paralleled the Hudson Division, but served largely a local patronage. The Harlem Division was much the more big-time, electrified as far as North White Plains and double-tracked to a point just beyond Brewster to accommodate the many commuter trains and occasional freights. The Putnam Division saw only local freights, and its commuter passenger runs were handled by 4-6-0s. A short branch connecting the two lines between Golden's Bridge, on the Harlem Line south of Brewster, and Lake Mahopac on the Putnam allowed some trains to use a cross-line routing.

(Above) Near Brewster Pacific 4642 is in charge of a Harlem Division run. Judging by the baggage car this train will proceed beyond Brewster. It's January 15, 1949; steam will last on the Harlem Division another 3 and a half years, ending in September, 1952.

(Left) On a drab March day in 1949 the 1255 is near Tilly Foster, just west of Brewster, with another Putnam Division run.

(Above and below) On the Putnam, which ran midway between the Harlem to the east and the Hudson Division mainline to the west, F-12 4-6-0 1274 is at Carmel, the Putnam County seat, on a sunny July 1, 1950. As the locomotive swings by Bill adds a portrait of the Ten Wheeler's engineer to his fine collection of crew pictures.

Nor did the Central confine itself to the east bank of the Hudson. Extending north from Weehawken, NJ, on the Hudson opposite New York, the line hugged the west bank of the Hudson for much of the way to Albany and connections at Selkirk Yard with the B&A and Mohawk Divisions. The West Shore's River Division in the Hudson Valley was much more oriented to freight traffic than the parallel Hudson Division, which lacked connections at New York City and which was clogged with passenger trains. There was a modest commuter service from Weehawken as far as Newburgh, and a few trains to Albany, but no name trains of the sort that graced the Hudson's east bank.

(Left) Freight Pacific 4459, class K-11, is near Newburgh with a local freight in March of 1949. The Central decided in the early Teens to standardize on 69" drivered 4-6-2s as its primary modern freight power, but soon found them too light for the rapidly expanding trains of the era, acquiring engines of the 4-8-2 and 2-8-2 types for its mainline freights. By then it had 200 freight Pacifics, and over the years used them much as other roads used 2-8-0s or light 2-8-2s, as the light road switchers of the steam era.

(Below) On March 16, 1941. Bill rode the West Shore in a thick river fog up the still icy river. He photographed one of the bridges near West Point along the way, in the stretch along the Hudson Highlands where the mountains close in on the river and the West Shore has to carve its way along the rocky shoreline.

(Above) Haverstraw, just over the state line in New York, was the terminus for many of the commuter runs on the West Shore. Two K-11 Pacifics, common power on West Shore commuter runs, are on the scene, with the 4551 entering town with a drab commuter train on a drab March 11, 1950.

(Below) One of the most famous locations on the lower Hudson Valley was the Bear Mountain Bridge, from which we see a Mohawk heading south about to pass under the graceful suspension bridge in the Hudson Highlands. Judging from the light angle it's midmorning of a hazy July 8, 1950.

Harmon, just a bit less than 33 miles north of Grand Central Station, assumed a position of critical importance for the Central in 1913, when third-rail electrification reached the village along the Hudson. All passenger trains changed engines here, a practice that lasted into diesel days, and a large shop, yard, and engine servicing facility was developed in recognition of Harmon's importance.

(Above) On July 30, 1950, Bill paid a memorable visit to Harmon. The Central was still in transition from steam to diesel power, and steam was still in abundance at Harmon. The station at Harmon was a favored spot for photographers to observe the action, as electrics dropped off their charges for steam and diesel power to take the Central's great passenger fleet northward along the Hudson. Hudson 5241 waits its turn as a Niagara prepares to head north on July 30, 1950.

(Below) Even though the Central possessed a modern roster of steam passenger units, diesel power had made great inroads by 1950, with most limiteds handled by two-unit sets of Es or the occasional Alco or FM cab power – even a few Baldwin units made a brief appearance. The E's were the victors, and who could argue with the aesthetics of units like E-7 4014 and its B unit mate, resplendent in its gray lightning stripe scheme and silvered trucks, waiting for the motor to bring its train up from Grand Central.

(Above) On the move at Harmon on the evening of July 30 is E-7 4000, the first of Central's 50 E-7s – 36 A's and 14 B's – with the COMMODORE VANDERBILT bound for Chicago's Lasalle Street Station. The 4000 features the small numberboards of early E-7s, requiring the large white numbers on the nose for identification purposes. It also sports a variation of the lightning stripe scheme with the stripe missing the characteristic lightning-bolt effect at the end of its body.

(Below) In the grand style of New York Central passenger service, the round-ended parlor-observation car brings up the rear of the train. Those individuals fortunate enough to find a seat near the end windows will enjoy perhaps the best scenery in the East, as the train speeds north in the evening along the "Rhineland of America." The COMMODORE VANDERBILT was second only to the TWENTIETH CENTURY LIMITED among the trains of the Central's Great Steel Fleet, an all-Pullman extra fare train. If it's on time, and there will be hell to pay if it isn't, it is 6:17 PM.

(Above and left) As the southern terminus of steam on the Hudson Division, Harmon's engine facility was among the busiest on the system. Bill's love of steam engines is evident in the care with which he recorded the variety of engines found at the double roundhouses at the Harmon engine terminal. Mohawk 2775 shows the effects of 25 years of hard service on the road of the Vanderbilts posing for Bill on July 30, 1950. The 2775 was one of the 100 4-8-2s of its class that the Central put to work in the late 1920s.

(Right) Also on hand that day was another class of the Mohawks, a class L-4a built by the Lima locomotive works in 1944. Engine 3104 employed some of the most state-of-the-art equipment available when built. With its Boxpok drivers, elephant ears, and improved counter-balancing the Central found these modern engines fitting to the needs of transporting goods to the Big Apple and ordered 50 such units in the depths of World War II.

(Above) Bill was able to find a rare treat in the form of chunky 0-8-0 7653 steaming away. Number 7653 belonged to class U-3b and was delivered to the Central in 1920. The diamond-shaped builder's plate identifies this as being an engine built by Lima at its Ohio locomotive works. By 1950 the 7653 is much worse for wear, with a rusty smokebox and firebox. With her small 51" drivers she was best suited for freight switching assignments.

(Below) We are now looking at Hudson 5451 poking its body out of one of the stalls at the Harmon roundhouse. Hudson 5451 was part of the Central's last order for Hudsons and was delivered in 1938. 5451 was also one of the ten engines that were delivered streamlined, in her case for the TWENTIETH CENTURY LIMITED. It has now lost its streamlined skirting and holds down less glamorous assignments as just another among the Central's 475 4-6-4s. It has the "Selkirk" front end shared with the L-4 Mohawks.

(Above) Bill found a surprisingly large number of Pacifics still in service on his trips to the Hudson Division of the NYC. July 30, 1950 was no exception. He was able to find Pacific 4709 taking a spin at the turntable with 5451's nose sticking out in the background.

(Below) Now both of the graceful Pacifics have coupled up together. Double-heading trains on the Hudson Division wasn't common, so chances are they're just preparing for a movement within the engine terminal area.

(Above) Pacific 4697 is steaming away on one of the many tracks in the engine terminal. Judging by the engineer's position it looks like the steamer is getting ready to make a back-up move.

(Below) Bill has now lensed a picture of the locomotives that gave Harmon its importance, the electrics. The Central found that a 600-volt direct current system on third rail pick-ups to be suitable to their needs. The line to Harmon was electrified between 1906 and 1913. S-2 class motor number 124 is shown at the Harmon shops. She's an old-timer, built by Alco-GE in 1906 and still going strong after 44 years of operation around New York City.

Let's finish our tour of Harmon with a look at the Niagaras. Entering service in the final months of the war, the Niagara was the ultimate steam power on the Central. In fact, nothing in the Northeast was even close to the state-of-the-art NYC 4-8-4s for power, speed, versatility, and modernity. The engines were designed to haul 20 car passenger trains at speeds up to 90 miles per hour and beyond. Designated class S-1, the Niagaras' only competition for the title of America's finest passenger steam engine could come from the Norfolk & Western's J-1s and the Union Pacific's 800s.

(Left) The 6001 displays her unique face for Bill on July 30, 1950. Only the ill-fated P&LE 2-8-4s looked anything like this, with the dual sealed-beam headlights (retrofitted a couple of years after delivery), flat Selkirk face, drop coupler, and smoke lifters. Like all of the Central's modern power, clearance restrictions demanded a compact look that accentuated the perfect balance of the design.

(Below) Harmon in the postwar years always had several Niagaras waiting to head back north to Albany and points west. The 6006 and 6001 sun themselves next to the roundhouse on July 30, 1950.

(Right) Looking at nearby 6007 from a tender-first angle, Bill was able to capture the majesty of the Niagara's massive PT-5 tender with its phenomenal coal capacity of 46 tons. These tenders dwarfed the J-3 Hudsons but looked just right with the Niagaras. Hostling engines at Harmon was dirty work, judging from the fellow on the 6007.

(Below) A look at 6001's running gear captures the power of these huge machines. The drivers are 79", up from the 75" that the first Niagara, the 6000, had on delivery. Belying their massive appearance was the emphasis the Central's designers had put on saving weight, including the light weight side rods with roller bearings visible in this shot.

(Above) Our final shot East of the Hudson, taken from the observation car of the LAURENTIAN bound for Montreal, shows FA-1 1043 on the point of a northbound freight being passed at Manitou, set against the mountains and the river that are so much a part of the Hudson Division . By this date, February 1953, the massive purchases of road switchers and cab units in the early 1950s have made steam an endangered species on the Hudson Division. That summer, on August 7, 1953, the 6020 will take the last steam train out of Harmon. In just a few years, as Robert Young and Alfred Perlman assume the leadership of the Central, even more fundamental change will affect this historic railroad: the four track mainline will be pared to two, the passenger fleet will dwindle in number and diminish in quality, the observation cars will no longer trail the matched consists of modern stainless-steel Budd cars. Thankfully, Bill McChesney was on hand to capture the great years of 1941-1953 on Kodachrome.

We hope you have shared the pleasure of being Trackside *with Bill McChesney.* Forthcoming volumes in the TRACKSIDE *series will allow you to share the experiences and vision of other great practitioners of the art of color photography as they bring to life those far-off days when railroads truly were the lifeblood of American commerce.*